ENCYCLOPEDIA OF MAMMALS

VOLUME 6
Gaz–Gui

MARSHALL CAVENDISH
NEW YORK • LONDON • TORONTO • SYDNEY

GAZELLES

RELATIONS

Duikers, dwarf antelopes, and gazelles belong to the order Artiodactyla and the family Bovidae. Other members of the family include:

GRAZING ANTELOPES

SPIRAL-HORNED ANTELOPES

FOUR-HORNED ANTELOPE

WILD CATTLE

DOMESTIC CATTLE

GOATS & SHEEP

Stan Osolinski/Oxford Scientific Films

NIMBLE HOOVES

LIGHT IN BUILD AND GRACEFUL IN MOVEMENT, THESE ARE THE MOST
DIMINUTIVE AND DAINTY OF THE HOOFED MAMMALS, CAPABLE OF
DARTING BENEATH THICK COVER OR RACING WITH NIMBLE STRIDES

Duikers, gazelles, and dwarf antelopes, such as the dik-dik *(above)*, are the featherweights of the world's hoofed mammals. Some of the beasts with which they share their ranges, such as buffalo, wildebeest, oryx, or mountain sheep, seem giants by comparison. Yet all these animals belong to the same family, the bovids. Duikers, gazelles, and dwarf antelopes, like the hefty buffalo, possess cleft hooves and a pair of horns, subsist on plant food, and have a complex digestive system.

But size and build most obviously set these three groups of herbivores apart from their assorted relatives. Few except the largest of the duikers stand higher than a man's waist, and most are slight in build. The smallest are tiny indeed: The shoulder height of the royal antelope is no greater than the length of a ruler (12 in/30 cm), and its head is the size of a small plum. Its close cousin, the pygmy antelope, is almost as small. And the slimmest of the gazelles, the gerenuk and the dibatag, achieve the epitome of

757

*A shy forager among Africa's lowland forests, the
blue duiker is one of the smallest of its tribe.*

Nigel Dennis/NHPA

slightness, with their long, slender legs, thin bodies,
and long necks. The dibatag stands at roughly the
same height as a fallow deer, yet the latter weighs
nearly three times more than this spindly gazelle.

Though less conspicuous than most of their relatives, duikers, dwarf antelopes, and gazelles are
highly successful animals, both in terms of abun-
dance and species diversity. Different species of
duikers occupy almost every stretch of closed forest
in Africa, while Thomson's gazelles are among the
most familiar animals on the East African plains.
Indeed, Africa has seventy-five bovid species in all,
and 50 percent of these are either duikers, dwarf
antelopes, or gazelles. Across the semideserts and
grasslands of Asia, a further six species of gazelles
range widely. Sadly most of them are much reduced
in number now, but they too were once among the
most abundant of herbivores in these arid habitats.

ANCESTRY

Today's dwarf antelopes may represent an ancient
lineage. Their body form is thought to have changed
little over the last 20 millon years; indeed, most of
the bovids, except the cattle, probably evolved from
dwarf antelopelike ancestors. All dwarf antelopes
are small, with females some 10–20 percent larger
than the males. With the exception of one race of
the crag-dwelling klipspringer, the males alone have
horns, and these are short, ringed spikes. Dwarf

758

Jen & Des Bartlett/Bruce Coleman Ltd.

CHEWING THE CUD

All bovids, along with deer and giraffes, are ruminants, or "chewers of the cud." Rechewing food is part of an elaborate digestive system that has evolved in these hoofed mammals to help them extract as many nutrients from plant food as possible.

Ruminants possess an enlarged stomach with four connecting chambers, each of which has a special role in breaking down the fibrous structure of tough plant parts and releasing the nutrients within. The rumen is the largest of the chambers and contains myriad microorganisms, which steadily work on swallowed food. Balls of food from the rumen are then regurgitated, rechewed with saliva, and sent back down to the next digestion chamber. The large storage capacity of the rumen and the ability to rechew food allows grazing and browsing animals to swallow large amounts of food quickly and then chew them more thoroughly later, perhaps in a safer place or in a posture that enables them to keep watch for danger.

antelopes have especially large scent glands in front of the eyes, and their coats vary from pale gray to dark brown.

Those species of dwarf antelopes that opt for open, savanna-like habitats—the steenbok, the grysbok, the oribi, and the beira—have an upright posture with a long neck. Those that live among scrub, thickets, and forests—the royal and pygmy antelopes, the suni, and the dik-diks—tend to have longer hind legs, an arched back, and a short neck, enabling them to dart under thick vegetation.

Duikers resemble the dwarf antelopes and share their preference for forest habitats. They were once regarded as having "primitive" characteristics, but this label is now doubted—for one thing, the duikers have the largest brains relative to body size of any antelope. Duikers made a highly successful evolutionary move, adapting both to a forest environment and to eating fallen fruit, a nutritious source of food unexploited by other forest-dwelling ruminants. They have evolved into a variety of species of small to middling size and with various colorations. Slightly stockier than dwarf antelopes, they also

Springbok and giraffe represent the rich diversity of form among grazers and browsers.

FEEDING NICHES

The ruminant digestive system confers several advantages upon herbivores. Not only does it extract more food value from herbage, but in the hind chambers any protein-rich stomach bacteria in the food is also digested. The bacteria can synthesize amino acids—the building blocks of protein—using nitrogen supplies that ruminants continually recycle rather than excrete.

This means that ruminants need not obtain all their vital amino acids from their food, allowing them more flexibility in diet. Ruminants are able to specialize more easily, and therefore more forms of them have evolved to exploit the full variety of herbivorous feeding niches. Today there are nearly six times as many living species of ruminant ungulates than nonruminants.

GAZELLES, SPRINGBOK, AND BLACKBUCK
Antilopini
(an-till-o-PEE-nee)

have larger heads, and both sexes generally bear short horns. Only one species, the common duiker, lives in more open habitats.

The earliest gazelle fossils date from about 14 million years ago, when the expanding grasslands and drylands in the Old World presented opportunities for herbivores that could feed in the open. Gazelles developed several traits that enabled them to do so, including the ability to conserve water in hot environments without overheating, the ability to survive better on fibrous grassy vegetation, and the acuteness of senses, the agility, and the running speed to evade predators in the absence of cover. Gazelles, in consequence, tend to be larger than duikers and dwarf antelopes, with longer legs and necks and slender bodies that give them a graceful appearance. Most have ringed, curving horns and a pelt ranging from pale fawn to dark brown, often with a dark flank marking and black and white stripes on the face. ■

DUIKERS
Cephalophini
(kef-al-o-FEE-nee)

The duikers, tribe Cephalophini, are small to medium-sized antelopes with a rounded back, high rump, short tail, and short, narrow horns present in both sexes. They are mainly forest-dwelling, although one species ranges widely across woodland savanna and bush. There are 17 species, all of which occur in sub-Saharan Africa.

B/W illustrations Ruth Grewcock

HIPPOS

PIGS

CAMELS

760

THE ANTELOPES' FAMILY TREE

The tribe Antilopini comprise 22 species distributed across Africa and through the dry heartland of Asia. Members of this tribe, which also includes the gerenuk, are small to medium-sized with a graceful, slender build, maximizing running speed. They are typified by long, equal-lengthed limbs and a straight back, long neck, and narrow muzzle. The tail is short to medium length. The heavily ringed horns vary from spikes to open S shapes and are usually present in both sexes. Gazelles inhabit open habitats from savanna and steppe to semidesert and desert proper.

Gazelles, dwarf antelopes, and duikers form part of a range of medium-sized to large mammals that possess hooves and also eat plant matter, known as the hoofed mammals or ungulates. There is still considerable debate over the divisions into families, subfamilies, and tribes, but the most basic distinction is between the odd-toed ungulates—horses, rhinoceroses, and tapirs—and the more numerous even-toed forms.

DWARF ANTELOPES

Neotragini
(nee-o-trag-EE-nee)

These are the smallest of the antelopes. Neotragini include the dik-dik, klipspringer, royal and suni antelope. They have a short tail, and males have short, spikelike horns. Females are slightly larger than males. They occur in forest, bush, savanna, and rocky habitats. There are 12 species in sub-Saharan Africa.

WILD CATTLE

GOATS AND SHEEP

SUBFAMILY ANTILOPINAE

GRAZING ANTELOPES

FAMILY BOVIDAE

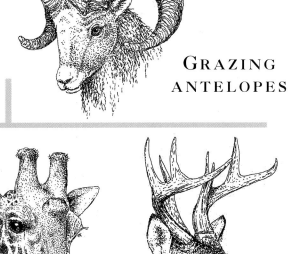

GIRAFFES

DEER

EVEN-TOED UNGULATES

ANATOMY:
THE SPRINGBOK

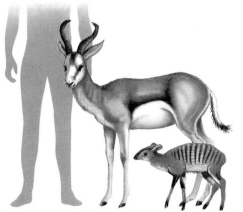

The largest of the gazelles, the dama gazelle, measures 57–68 in (145–172 cm) from head to rump, whereas the springbok (above left) is a medium-sized gazelle. The striped-back duiker (above right) is approximately 40 in (100 cm) long, while the royal antelope is the smallest antelope at about 22.5 in (575 mm) in length and about 4.5 lb (2 kg) in weight.

HORNS

The curving shape, outward spread, and ringed ridges of the springbok's horns are typical of gazelles. Those of males, which engage in sparring bouts especially at mating time, are thicker and more curved. The curves and rings help rivals lock horns, making fights more of a head wrestle than a stabbing match.

THE LIMBS

are fine and fragile in appearance, but they are structured so as to minimize weight and maximize anchorage for those muscles that provide speed and jumping power—like those of a human sprinter or hurdler.

THE COAT COLOR

of most duiker species is subdued, in a range of bluish grays and dull browns. Stripes add to the camouflaging effect and help to hide the animal in thickets of ground cover.

STRIPED-BACK DUIKER

A duiker, with its humped back, shorter neck, and shorter legs, has a much more compact, crouched build than the typical gazelle. A low profile and well-developed hind legs help the animal push its way rapidly through densely vegetated habitats.

PYGMY ANTELOPE

The skeletal profile reveals the slightness of a pygmy antelope's build. The limb bones are long and fine, giving the animal a ballerina-like agility and grace of movement.

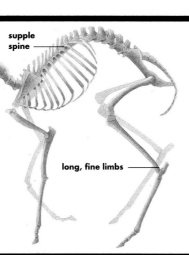

supple spine

long, fine limbs

SKULL
The lightweight skull of a common duiker features large eye sockets placed well to the sides, showing the importance of keen peripheral vision for an animal that relies mainly on early warning and running speed to evade predators.

COMMON DUIKER

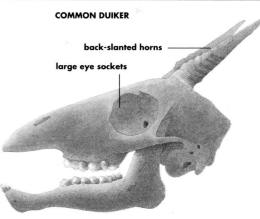

back-slanted horns

large eye sockets

The horns of a male salt dik-dik are tiny but lethally sharp; they are angled backward.

The klipspringer's horns, like those of the dik-dik, are short and sharp. They are used almost exclusively in defense.

The gerenuk's S-shaped horns are used both as stabbing rapiers and as battering rams. The thick bases also protect the skull. The ridges lock with an enemy's horns to prevent him from launching a stabbing attack.

CLASSIFICATION

GENUS: *ANTIDORCAS*

SPECIES: *MARSUPIALIS*

SIZE

HEAD–BODY LENGTH: 48–56 IN (120–140 CM)

SHOULDER HEIGHT: 27–34 IN (70–87 CM)

TAIL LENGTH: 8–11 IN (20–28 CM)

HORNS: 14–19 IN (35–48 CM)

WEIGHT: 55–100 LB (25–45 KG)

COLORATION

CINNAMON-BROWN UPPER PARTS

DARK BROWN BAND ACROSS FLANKS

WHITE TAIL, UNDERSIDE, AND RUMP

FEATURES

SLENDER BUILD

NARROW, ELONGATED MUZZLE

LONG LEGS

LONG NECK

CURVING, RINGED HORNS

RAISABLE PALE CREST ON RUMP

DARK STRIPES ALONG SIDES OF FACE

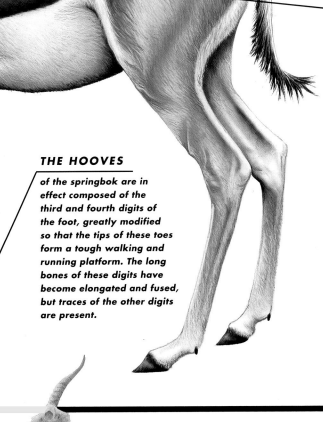

COAT

The springbok is one of several gazelles that possess a prominent dark stripe along the flank. The stripe may have the effect of helping to break up the animal's outline in a tight herd. Alternatively it may function in a short range as a prominent social signal to other members of the herd, and its movement in a bolting gazelle may instantly communicate alarm.

THE HOOVES

of the springbok are in effect composed of the third and fourth digits of the foot, greatly modified so that the tips of these toes form a tough walking and running platform. The long bones of these digits have become elongated and fused, but traces of the other digits are present.

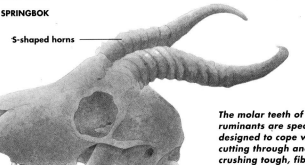

THOMSON'S GAZELLE

Like all gazelles, the "tommy" is built for speed—it can outrun all predators but the cheetah—although it lacks stamina. Its capacity for speed is reflected in the lightweight, open skeleton (left).

long limbs for high speed

SPRINGBOK

S-shaped horns

upper incisors absent

shearing molars

The molar teeth of ruminants are specially designed to cope with cutting through and crushing tough, fibrous vegetation. Neatly shaped cusps on the teeth provide shearing edges for this purpose.

Main illustration Kim Thompson. Head comparisons Ruth Grewcock

EVER ON THE ALERT

WITH THE THREAT OF PREDATION EVER PRESENT, THE NEED TO REMAIN WATCHFUL AND ALERT IS A CONSTANT ELEMENT IN THE FEEDING, SOCIAL, AND REPRODUCTIVE BEHAVIOR OF THESE TIMID HERBIVORES

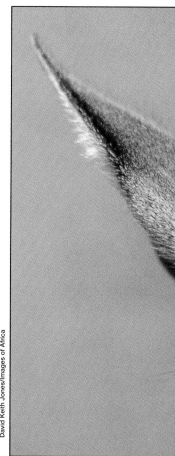

B oldness is not a quality normally associated with duikers, dwarf antelopes, and gazelles. These more or less delicately built herbivores are of a size that makes them favored prey for a long list of carnivores. Across their various habitats and ranges, adults or fawns are preyed on by lions, tigers, leopards, cheetahs, servals, caracals, black bears, wolves, hunting dogs, foxes, jackals, hyenas, civets, wild boars, baboons, pythons, monitor lizards, large owls, vultures, and eagles. Not surprisingly, one of the most obvious facets of their behavior is their natural timidity and alertness to danger. Their bearing while foraging betrays their fear: either quick and nervy as in most of the duikers, or slow and cautious as in most gazelles. Possessed of keen hearing and smell, as well as excellent wide-angle eyesight, they are always poised for evasive action.

POWERED BY ITS LONG HIND LIMBS, A ROYAL ANTELOPE CAN JUMP TWICE ITS HEIGHT AND SIX TIMES ITS LENGTH

For the gazelles, which live primarily in wide-open habitats and rely on vision for early detection of predators, the safest time for feeding and other activities is during daylight. They are generally at their most active early and late in the day, and none are truly nocturnal. Nevertheless, all undertake some movements and limited bouts of foraging from time to time at night.

Dwarf antelopes are more even in their spread of activity. They tend to alternate sessions of feeding with periods of rumination throughout the day and into the night, although they too show some peaking of activity in early morning and late afternoon. Duikers show the most diversity in their activity patterns. For example, the bay duiker is wholly

nocturnal, the yellow-backed duiker may forage both by day and by night, and the black-fronted duiker is one of several that are active solely by day. The diurnal species hide at night on the forest floor, often under logs or among tree roots.

All the duikers that forage by day share a rapid, nervous style of movement as they progress with heads low through the forest understory. When startled, they dash forward and leap across obstacles with body full stretched, then plunge into cover.

Springbok often leap to signal danger (above)*; this gesture is called stotting or pronking.*

David Keith Jones/Images of Africa

Thomas Dressler/Planet Earth Pictures

TAKING THE HEAT

Given the harshness of some of their habitats, it is not only the dangers of predation that test the survival of gazelles: The environment presents threats of its own. Yet gazelles are among the most tolerant of mammals, especially of high temperatures. Those that live around the Sahara and the Arabian deserts—such as the dorcas and dama gazelles—can cope with daytime temperatures up to 113°F (45°C). They allow their own body temperature to rise as air temperature rises, sometimes by as much as twenty degrees. Grant's gazelle of East Africa even allows its body to heat up a few degrees above air temperature. It is one of the few animals that remains active on the plains during the intense heat of midday.

Their very name is Afrikaans for the word *diver* and refers to the way they escape into undergrowth. Royal antelopes and dik-diks have a similar walking posture and are equally darting and bounding in their dash for cover.

The oribi and the steenbok have a much more upright posture, which suits them better for the sustained running that their more open habitat demands. To reach cover, they are usually forced to traverse a greater distance. For gazelles, sprinting ability is paramount, since outrunning attackers may be the only course open. All have an erect posture whether walking, trotting, or running, and when moving at full speed they can make leaps of several yards. Smaller gazelles increase their speed by taking very quick but full strides, with phases when all four limbs are off the ground and fully outstretched.

With the exception of the gerenuk and the dibatag, which tend to live alone or in twos and threes, gazelles are gregarious animals associating mainly in small herds of perhaps ten or so individuals. Larger groupings of Grant's and Thomson's gazelles and springbok occur on the plains of Africa, and blackbuck occur in India, but on a much lesser scale than in the past because of shrinking populations. In a few locations Thomson's gazelles and springbok still aggregate in loose herds of a few thousand. Dwarf antelopes and duikers, by contrast, are much less sociable, living in small family parties, pairs, or in some cases singly. ∎

The bush duiker's long ears are highly sensitive, and its eyes give excellent peripheral vision.

HABITATS

These herbivores inhabit an astounding range of environments. Gazelles in particular span several climatic zones, from the southern tip of Africa, with its cool winters; across the forests, plains, and deserts of tropical Africa, North Africa, Arabia, and India; and into the arid steppes of China and Mongolia, where winters are bitterly cold.

Apart from the common duiker, which prefers bush and open woodland, all the duikers dwell in areas of dense cover—mainly forest, but also on wooded riversides, in thickets on savannas, and in tall grass. Several species, including the zebra duiker, Peter's duiker, and Abbot's duiker, occur in montane forest at altitudes of up to 12,800 ft (4,000 m). Some—including the white-bellied duiker, the black duiker, and the red-flanked duiker—prefer forest edges to the deep, dark interior of large forests, while the black-fronted duiker is found in swampy forests.

Among the dwarf antelopes, the royal and pygmy antelopes both inhabit lush forest habitats in Africa, while the suni lives in smaller forest and

Thomson's gazelle is ideally suited to open plains, where its speed helps it escape predators.

David Keith Jones/Images of Africa

FOCUS ON

TSAVO NATIONAL PARK, KENYA

At over 8,000 sq mi (20,000 sq km) in area, Tsavo is Kenya's largest and wildest national park. Located toward the coast and bisected by the Nairobi–Mombasa railroad, the park is a dry, sparsely peopled wilderness, particularly toward the east. To the west, the plains are more dotted with low bushes, acacias, and baobab trees, framed against lines of rugged mountains. Yet everywhere the rich red soil shows through, not just on the ground but coating the hides of the park's elephant herds.

Here can be seen ostriches, buffalo, zebras, hartebeests, and warthogs, which all gather at dusk around water holes. The park is also a stronghold for the scarce gerenuk gazelle. Lions live here, along with leopards, genets, and mongooses. Verraux's eagles make breathtaking passes along stony crags inhabited by klipspringers, and the park's abundant bird life also includes several species of hornbills.

Stan Osolinski/Oxford Scientific Films

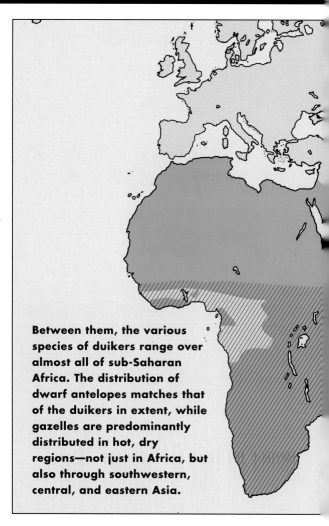

Between them, the various species of duikers range over almost all of sub-Saharan Africa. The distribution of dwarf antelopes matches that of the duikers in extent, while gazelles are predominantly distributed in hot, dry regions—not just in Africa, but also through southwestern, central, and eastern Asia.

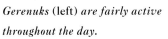

Gerenuks (left) *are fairly active throughout the day.*

thickets outside the main rain-forest regions. Dik-diks favor fairly dry country with evergreen, shrubby ground cover. More open habitats with scattered trees and shrubs are home to the oribi, the steenbok, and the grysbok, while the beira dwells in dry, barren hills and mountains in the Horn of Africa.

The widespread klipspringer turns up almost wherever there are rocky outcrops with bushes as cover. It is well adapted for life among the rocks, cliffs, and massifs. Strong hind limbs help it negotiate slopes, and it can stand securely with hooves close together on tiny ledges. Its hoof tips wear down more rapidly on the inside, leaving ridges around the rim that give the animal better traction.

Gazelles are closely associated with open habitats such as savannas, steppes, and deserts, though Grant's gazelle may also be seen in lightly wooded country. Often their habitats have scant vegetation and stony or sandy ground. The relief is often hilly or mountainous, and the Tibetan gazelle occupies plateau land up to 19,200 ft (6,000 m) above sea level.

Several attributes fit gazelles for life in the bleak and open, including speed, stamina, and, for some, resistance to the cold. Perhaps their most impressive feature is their ability to withstand hot desert conditions. The slender-horned, dama, goitered, and dorcas gazelles all inhabit regions of the Sahara and Arabia, where they roam in search of plants. They conserve moisture by producing concentrated urine and dry feces and by minimizing sweating. When they need to cool off, they do so by panting through the nose with closed mouth—a process that wastes relatively little moisture. ∎

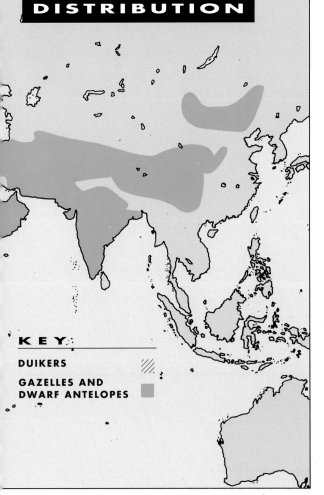

DISTRIBUTION

KEY

DUIKERS

GAZELLES AND
DWARF ANTELOPES

Unlike most gazelles, Grant's gazelle (below) *often lives in wooded or marshy habitats.*

DEFENSES

Duikers, dwarf antelopes, and gazelles react with suspicion to the sight, sound, or smell of anything new entering their vicinity. Standing still with head held high and alert, they rapidly assess the threat. What happens next depends on the species, the terrain, how far away an enemy is, and whether it has yet spotted its prey. Thomson's gazelles out on the plain may actually move toward an intruder to keep a check on its movements. If the animal is not actively stalking them, their usual response is then to maintain a safe distance. For a speedy cheetah this would be no less than 1,000 ft (300 m).

In the forest, a duiker is likely to freeze first on detecting danger, often in midstride, and if not yet spotted will either sink down into the undergrowth or sneak quietly into cover. In forested, bushy, or tall-grass habitats, dwarf antelopes tend to do likewise. Both the steenbok and the oribi lie prone in cover, with ears folded down.

Often, the hidden animal escapes detection. But if the predator flushes or stumbles upon the animal, or if it is suprised while grazing, immediate and swift escape is vital. Duikers dash away with a dodging run and plunge into thickets. Steenboks burst from their refuge and race into another patch of cover, while the oribi sprints off, often stopping after 650 ft (200 m) or so to look back and reassess the threat.

Living in a forest environment, a zebra duiker, or striped-back duiker, relies upon its cryptic patterning to conceal it from predators (left).

PRONKING

Springbok under attack from a predator (below) *are likely to react by leaping 7 ft (2 m) high, each animal bounding in a different direction before racing off. This curious habit is known as pronking.*

inSIGHT

CAMOUFLAGE

The coats of duikers, dwarf antelopes, and gazelles provide various degrees of camouflage in different ways. Most of the open-country species have fawn or pale brown coloring, making them especially difficult to spot from afar through the haze of daytime heat over pallid, arid terrain. A countershading of pale brown above neatly demarcated from white beneath may also have the effect of breaking up the animal's outline at a distance. In many forest duikers, such cryptic coloration is strongly developed. Stripes across the back of the zebra duiker and the contrastingly black head and neck of Jentink's duiker probably help to break up these animals' outlines amid dense vegetation.

When an attack is imminent, gazelles similarly take to their heels, dashing across plains, leaping obstacles, and scaling slopes with wonderful speed and agility. Blackbuck, springbok, and Thomson's gazelles can sprint at over 50 mph (80 km/h)—speed they need to keep ahead of a cheetah before it tires. Should the cat close, a fleeing gazelle will zigzag sharply to exhaust the pursuer. Though slower, wolf packs, hyenas, and wild dogs are more enduring and therefore more deadly enemies.

A striking feature of gazelles and of some dwarf antelopes is their habit of stotting while fleeing—making a series of high, bold bounds with legs held straight. It is usually combined with a raising of the white rump hairs. This habit reaches its extreme in the springbok, whose especially lofty, accentuated bounding is known as pronking. Whether these reactions provide a better view, confuse or bewilder predators, or simply raise an alarm is uncertain.

Alarm-raising is a key part in the defense of duikers and dwarf antelopes. Those duikers that live in close family groups, such as Maxwell's duiker, stamp their hind feet to warn their kin of danger. Dwarf antelopes and duikers whistle and snort. Dik-diks and klipspringers utter sharp whistles when first alarmed and utter further alarm calls when they have reached a safe distance. Gazelles twitch the skin on their flanks just before bolting, a subtle signal detected by others in the herd and highly visible in those species with flank stripes. ■

Robin Boutell/Wildlife Art Agency

FOOD AND FEEDING

Gazelles, dwarf antelopes, and duikers feed on the greenest, most tender and nutritious plant parts they can find. Relatively small, they can live on food sources too sparse to support bigger herbivores, which have to fill up on rough herbage. But there is another side to the coin. Small animals burn up food energy more rapidly than their larger counterparts, so they need to maximize the amount of nutrients contained in each mouthful eaten.

For forest duikers, choice food comes mainly in the form of wild fruit, which is usually lower in sugar and higher in protein. This can account for 75 percent of the diet of the minuscule blue duiker. The remainder consists of leaves, shoots, buds, flowers, and fungi. Big fruits can be tackled by the larger species, although such food is generally scarce. The common duiker feeds mainly on leaves, seeds, and flowers, although its fondness for fruit is evident in the way it stretches up on its hind legs to pluck it.

Duikers forage intensively but cautiously. They root through the leaf litter to reveal fruit and other items, and stretch up to pull down foliage with their

Anthony Bannister/NHPA

EATING UP

The gerenuk is unusual among gazelles in its almost wholesale concentration on eating the shrub foliage. To improve its access to fresh leaves, it can stand erect on its hind legs and actually walk two-legged around acacia bushes (right).

Small fruits; fresh, juicy growing tips; and tender leaves are the mainstay of the common duiker's diet (left).

Illustration Evi Antoniou

long tongues. A relatively large gape enables them to swallow fruit and other bulky objects and also gives their jaws greater power. Their cheek teeth can deal with roots and bark, and they may also eat rotting wood. From time to time, all species probably take some animal food, such as insects, snails, eggs, and even the occasional small vertebrate.

The fact that the duiker's diet is relatively scarce means that a given area of forest cannot support many animals. This favors solitary foraging or foraging in small groups only and prompts the defense of good feeding sites within well-marked territories.

The tiny royal and pygmy antelopes eat the youngest and juiciest parts of foliage, as well as fungi, buds, seeds, and small fruit. Dwarf antelopes are highly selective in their food, and, like the duikers, they are seldom sociable and tend to defend their feeding resources, whatever the habitat.

The small jaws and muzzles of dwarf antelopes enable them to glean between old leaves and twigs to select only the most nutritious morsels and to nip tiny young leaves or seeds from the ground level without eating coarser material at the same time. The fine snout of the dik-dik acts almost like forceps in picking off the smallest morsel. Dik-diks also trap food with their minute tongues.

Besides dense vegetation, dwarf antelopes such as steenboks, grysboks, klipspringers, and beiras eat a mixture of shrubs, herbs, and, to a lesser extent, grasses. There is one exception: The oribi is chiefly a grazer. Though it browses to some extent, especially in the dry season, it mainly eats green grass. It is especially fond of the fresh shoots that spring up after a fire and is one of the first antelopes to find food on charred ground.

in SIGHT

LOW LIQUID LOSS

Gazelles are renowned for their ability to manage on very little drinking water, even in baking, semidesert environments. Though some visit water holes, especially in the dry season, most species gain the bulk of their water needs through their food. Succulents are of particular value since they have special water-storage tissues as an adaptation to arid climates, but gazelles can also gain sufficient water from fresh leaves of other plants, particularly the young, juicy ones. The dorcas, red-fronted, slender-horned, Grant's, and Speke's gazelles all have exceedingly low drinking-water requirements, and the gerenuk and dibatag may never drink at all.

Among the gazelles, grazing is more common. Some, particularly Thomson's gazelles, depend on grasses and associated herbs; most others eat a mixture of grasses, herbs, and shrub foliage, along with shoots and fruits. Gazelles eat whatever is fresh, suitable, and available. The springbok grazes when grasses and herbs are in the flush of new growth, but turns to the leaves of low shrubs and succulents later in the season. But gazelles are choosy eaters: Their narrow muzzles and flexible lips are excellent tools for selecting the most tender parts of plants, and they can find enough such food even among the scant, scattered plant life of the desert fringes.

THOMSON'S GRAZERS

Most gazelles rely on a mixture of grass, herbs, and foliage. Thomson's gazelle (below) *grazes more than most, and during the rainy season large herds of these graceful animals occupy short-grass plains where few other sources of food are available.*

Heads down at a Kalahari water hole, springboks keep a watchful eye out for roving big cats.

Because grasses and herbs are often locally abundant, defending food resources is much less of a priority among gazelles. This helps to explain why gazelles are much less tied to territory and are much more sociable than duikers and dwarf antelopes. In many drier regions gazelles are nomadic. Nomadism allows species like the dorcas gazelle to find the short-lived patches of green growth that spring up after dry-season storms. Gazelles also make regular seasonal migrations in search of better or more sheltered pasture, sometimes gathering en masse before the great trek. Dama gazelles follow the rains into the southern fringes of the Sahara, while goitered, Tibetan, and Mongolian gazelles migrate to lower altitudes in winter to avoid the worst weather. Huge numbers of Thomson's gazelles, along with wildebeest, and zebras, make up the famous migrating hordes of the Serengeti plains. ■

P. Perry/Frank Lane Picture Agency

ANIMAL SNACKS

Proteins are essential constituents of an animal's body. Some are the main building blocks of body tissue; others control the animal's physiology. When animals eat, they break down the proteins in their food, absorb the amino acids that result, and reassemble them into the particular proteins they require.

Plant food is fairly low in protein. Larger hoofed mammals can utilize proteins produced by their own stomach bacteria, but smaller ungulates sometimes need the extra boost that only protein-rich animal food can provide. Hence about 0.5 percent of a duiker's diet consists of carnivorous snacks, such as ants and caterpillars and even small vertebrates such as lizards. Captive duikers have even been known to catch and eat small birds and mice.

Illustration Peter David Scott/Wildlife Art Agency

TERRITORY

Virtually all duikers, dwarf antelopes, and gazelles defend living spaces to some degree, but their territorial habits vary. Duikers and dwarf antelopes tend to occupy small, well-bounded, permanent territories, while among the gazelles the use of space is much more fluid and strict territoriality is confined to males during breeding periods. The differences are due to distinctions in habitat and food resources.

LAW OF THE JUNGLE

Living mainly in forests and bushy terrain has several implications for the sociability of duikers and dwarf antelopes. It means that rich food resources are quite plentiful but concentrated in pockets, such as fruiting trees and shrubs with new foliage; this favors intimate knowledge of a small area. The ready availability of cover also favors concealment as a means of evading predators.

Once individuals have found a living space, they tend to stay put, regularly marking boundaries with scent and excreta and driving out intruders. Mates may form monogamous bonds and live together on a territory with some of their young, or they may mate freely with territorial neighbors. So a pair of blue duikers, plus one or two immature young, will hold a

> CONFLICT IS RARE IN STABLE DUIKER GROUPS, OTHER THAN WHEN INTRUDERS FAIL TO OBSERVE TERRITORIAL BORDERS

territory of less than ten acres (four hectares). Dik-diks live in similar groups but in a larger territory. A male oribi may share a territory of 250 acres (100 hectares) usually with one but sometimes with a few adult females, while a male pygmy antelope's territory usually overlaps those of at least two females.

OUT IN THE OPEN

Plains-dwelling gazelles lead very different social lives. Their grazing and browsing resources are more evenly distributed and abundant, but also subject to seasonal scarcity. Adopting small, fixed territories is less valuable in terms of securing resources, so many species migrate or wander nomadically. Moreover, living in larger groups on the grasslands is not only viable, because good pasture can support a higher density of animals, but also more secure, because herds provide safety in numbers in the open.

Blackbuck males resolve breeding rights with a ritualized clashing of horns.

Priscilla Barratt/Wildlife Art Agency

Vivek Sinha/Survival Anglia

HEAD-TO-HEAD

Rival male Grant's gazelles use ritual threats ranging from a head-up stance with horns laid back (above) to a head-down posture with horns to the fore.

INSIGHT

HORN VARIETY

Horns vary greatly between duikers and dwarf antelopes on the one hand and gazelles on the other. In the first two groups, horns are little more than short, straight spikes, either stubby or narrow at the base. But an upward blow from them can be a stab for self-defense or a lethal way to settle a rare fight.

In gazelles, fighting between rival males is so common that elaborate horns have evolved as a means of minimizing lethal blows. Gazelle horns tend not only to be bigger, but also to have circular ridges and twisted shapes. Such horns are designed to lock together in combat, leaving the rivals to head-wrestle rather than stab—although now and again mortal wounds do occur.

Social behavior among gazelles is in general complex, showing most clearly in rituals of dominance and submission between males. Aggression is rife because of the mating potential that high status and the chance to take hold of a territory can bring. Rival male gazelles may resort to ritualized fighting—butting, pushing, and head-wrestling with horns interlocked—until one animal beats a retreat.

Intermale aggression is so important in male gazelles in establishing the right to breed that evolution has favored powerful males with imposing horns. Male gazelles are on average both larger and longer-horned than females; indeed, most female Asian gazelles lack horns. In dwarf antelopes and duikers, though, the sexes look similar and the females are often slightly larger. ∎

Outside the mating season, then, mixed herds of gazelles are the norm, but at breeding times these break down into groups of females with recent young and groups of nonbreeding males, while mature males establish temporary territories. Each single territorial male tries to mate with any receptive female in his patch and is often accompanied by a female herd for some time. But scent marks and excreta, along with threat displays involving brandishing of horns and horning of vegetation, are all employed to repel rival males. Territory size varies considerably from under one acre (0.4 hectares) in some populations of Thomson's gazelles to as much as 850 acres (340 hectares) in the gerenuk.

MESSAGE SCENT

Rubbing scent from a gland in front of its eye onto plants helps a dik-dik lay claim to its territory (right). All dwarf antelopes, duikers, and gazelles have this gland.

LIFE CYCLE

Compared with some other aspects of their behavior, the breeding habits of duikers, dwarf antelopes, and gazelles are broadly similar. In tropical zones at least, breeding is not tied to any single time of the year. Nevertheless, distinct birth peaks occur, especially in savanna species, with mating periods timed so that more young are born during food flushes that coincide with one or two bouts of seasonal rains. Outside the tropics, in those regions of Central Asia that experience harsh winter cold, gazelles give birth in the spring.

In all species, courtship tends to be initiated by the male. A male duiker begins by following his partner until he has a chance to sniff her urine and discover whether or not she is about to come into estrus. If she is, he becomes even more persistent over the next few days, even turning to chasing and butting, until she becomes receptive and willing to mate. A similar pattern, differing only in details of the ritual, occurs with gazelles and dwarf antelopes. Courtship sometimes involves vocalizations, such as a growling sound produced by male dorcas gazelles.

A series of short mating sessions occur for up to a day between partners, followed by several months of pregnancy for the female. When a female gazelle is ready to give birth, she typically moves away from the herd to a concealed site where she delivers her single fawn. Though newborn duikers, dwarf antelopes, and gazelles are quite well developed, all of them spend the first weeks of life lying low in bushes or tall grass, scarcely moving unless the mothers return to suckle them. And though the mothers may be with them for no more than one or two hours per day, this concealment strategy is the youngs' best means of defense from predators during this highly vulnerable stage. In those duikers and dwarf antelopes that live in stable pairs, males may assist in parental care by being extra vigilant for predators and by responding to fawns' distress calls. But otherwise tending to the concealed youngster is done by the female.

GAINING GROUND

The male may one day acquire enough strength and experience to fight for the takeover of a territory (below).

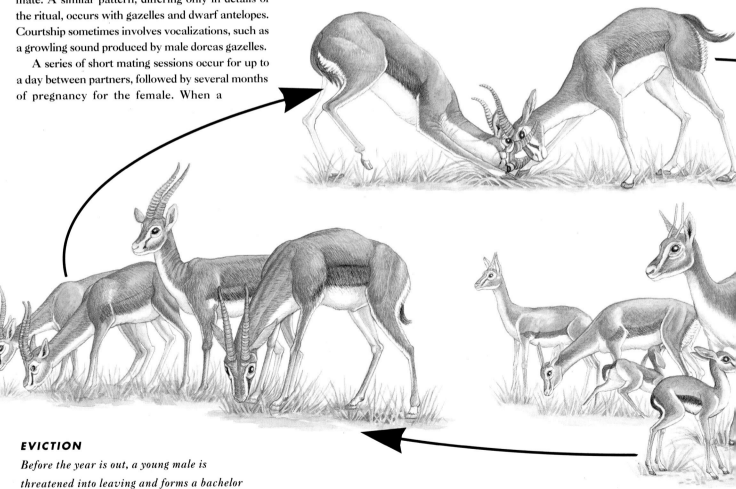

EVICTION

Before the year is out, a young male is threatened into leaving and forms a bachelor group with other young males (above).

in SIGHT

LYING OUT

The young of duikers, dwarf antelopes, and gazelles all spend their first few weeks concealed in cover—a behavior called lying out. Lacking any odor and staying still lessens the chances of their being detected by enemies. In addition, they are hard to spot against the ground. In several of the duikers, the newborns lack the bolder colors of their parents; hence the yellow rump of the yellow-backed duiker is entirely absent for the first month of life. Both Jentink's duiker and the bay duiker are born darker brown than adults and lack, respectively, the adults' black hood and black stripe along the back.

David Keith Jones/Images of Africa

Cryptic colors and body shape combine superbly to conceal a gazelle fawn.

GROWING UP

The life of a Thomson's gazelle

READY TO MATE

Having avoided a male's advances until her time is due, a female Thomson's gazelle at last allows him to mount (right). Six months later she moves away from the herd to a secret refuge and gives birth to a single young.

IN THE NURSERY

For several weeks the offspring lies in hiding, moving only when summoned for milk by its mother. At several months old the young is developed enough to run with the herd (right).

At about the time of weaning, a few months after birth, fawns begin foraging with their mothers, and mother and offspring gazelles become reintegrated into a herd. The youngster is still very vulnerable, but at least it is learning how to spot danger and flee. Those young that survive the early months develop rapidly, and by the first or second year may already have reached sexual maturity.

Duikers and dwarf antelopes tend to strike out on their own during the second year; males are often forced by their fathers to leave earlier than females, which may be tolerated in the family group even when fully adult. In male klipspringers, the first signs of harrassment by the father may begin as soon as the horns start to appear, at about six months.

In gazelles, young females may remain close by their mothers for a year before taking their place within the herd. Young males, however, are apt to be displaced by territorial males as early as eight months and forced to join bachelor herds. ∎

FROM BIRTH TO DEATH

THOMSON'S GAZELLE
BREEDING: YEAR ROUND. BIRTHS AND MATING PEAK DURING THE RAINS AND 6 MONTHS LATER
GESTATION: 6 MONTHS
LITTER SIZE: USUALLY 1
REJOINS HERD: 10 WEEKS
WEANING: 3–6 MONTHS
SEXUAL MATURITY: FROM 1 YEAR IN MALES AND FEMALES

BLUE DUIKER
BREEDING: THROUGHOUT THE YEAR
GESTATION: 4 MONTHS
LITTER SIZE: 1
REJOINS HERD: 4 WEEKS
WEANING: 2–3 MONTHS
SEXUAL MATURITY: FROM 1 YEAR IN MALES AND FEMALES

Illustrations Carol Roberts

ABUNDANCE PAST

THE INCREASING AVAILABILITY OF GUNS, MORE THAN ANYTHING ELSE, HAS SET GAZELLES, DWARF ANTELOPES, AND DUIKERS ON A COURSE OF DECLINE THAT CONTINUES TO THIS DAY

Not so long ago, gazelles provided some of nature's greatest wildlife spectacles. Across Africa and much of Asia, they numbered among the most abundant of the larger mammals and were found in barren habitats shunned by other species. In the later 19th century, herds of 10,000 or more blackbuck roamed on prime grasslands in India, and vast herds of springbok were still making sporadic mass migrations in southern Africa. Such treks at times involved hundreds of thousands of animals, and their passing could take days.

Today the only comparable spectacle is provided by the seasonal migrations of several thousand Thomson's gazelles in the Serengeti. All gazelles have declined over the last century or two—in many cases to a tragic extent. Various pressures have been to blame, and none more so than hunting.

Gazelles have highly palatable flesh, and their speed makes them exciting to hunt. Hunting for both food and sport has a long history, stretching back to prehistoric times. Ancient stone corrals in Israel were used as pens into which wild gazelles were driven. Indian nobility once used tame cheetahs for hunting blackbuck, and falcons have also been used to impede gazelles being chased by dogs.

But it was the development of rifles, and later of off-road vehicles, that really sent gazelles into decline. Since the early 19th century and especially in the 20th century, firearms have become widespread in many regions where gazelles live. The results have been devastating, and nowhere more so than in the arid lands around the Sahara, in the Horn of Africa, and in southwest Asia.

Almost all the gazelles of these deserts and semi-deserts have been decimated in range and number. Naturally more scarce because of the aridity of their habitat, they are also easier to track from vehicles because of the nature of the terrain. The red gazelle of Algeria was already extinct by the 1900s, and the dama gazelle, extinct over most of its range in the southern Sahara, remains threatened in the few pockets where it survives. Similar tales can be told for the dorcas, goitered, mountain, red-fronted, slender-horned, Soemmerring's, Speke's, and Cuvier's gazelles. Still, today, new pressures arise. Recent reports tell of intensive poaching of Mongolian gazelles for their meat, some of which is exported to Europe, and for their horns, which are being sold in parts of Asia as a substitute for rhino horn.

Carlo Dani & Ingrid Jeske/Natural Science Photos

The dama gazelle, which once roamed a vast range over the southern Sahara, is now at risk (above).

Mary Clay/Planet Earth Pictures

THEN & NOW

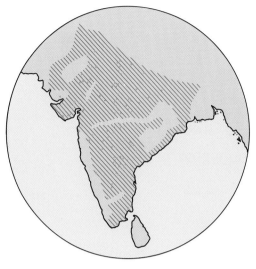

This map shows the decline of the range of the blackbuck over the last century.

FORMER DISTRIBUTION   CURRENT DISTRIBUTION

The blackbuck's decline has been simply catastrophic. This elegant, beautiful gazelle was once found almost all over India; estimates of its numbers in the 19th century stand at about four million. But hunting, which for this gazelle has a long history, began affecting the population from the late 1940s. With looser gun laws and the use of jeeps, hunters penetrated even the most remote areas.

The massacre was swift. Within a few years the blackbuck was already becoming extinct in former strongholds; it vanished completely in Pakistan and Bangladesh. By the early 1960s, the entire population of blackbuck had been wiped out from all but a string of isolated sites across India.

Duikers and dwarf antelopes too are subject to hunting pressures, which in some areas are severe. Duikers are widely hunted for their meat in forested areas, often with the use of lights at night, which dazzle and confuse the animals. The suni, the oribi, and the klipspringer are likewise hunted for their meat, while the dik-dik's skin is reportedly used in some regions for making garments such as gloves. Uncontrolled hunting in the 20th century has probably had its most dramatic impact on blackbuck and

Hunters used to obtain permits to kill blackbuck on the false pretext that their crops were at risk.

779

Kenneth W. Fink/Ardea

First described by zoologists in 1892, Jentink's duiker is now probably the rarest of all duikers.

antelopes, and duikers. Settlement in lowlands and valleys of Central Asia, for example, has barred goitered gazelles from many of their former winter refuges. Forest clearance has fragmented the distribution of many duikers, such as the red duiker in eastern and southern Africa, and especially those duikers such as the zebra and black duikers that occur in the dwindling rain forests of West Africa.

Even where pastoral farming maintains a similar habitat, as in the use of open savannas for grazing, wild animals are likely to lose their food resources and be ousted—if they do not succumb first to transmissible livestock diseases such as rinderpest. More commonly, large estates and ranches are likely to be fenced off, breaking up and isolating wild herds and preventing species like the springbok from migrating and ensuring an adequate food supply.

Some species are especially vulnerable to extinction from hunting or habitat destruction because they have a naturally limited distribution and low overall population. Ader's duiker, which is restricted to the Tanzanian island of Zanzibar and one coastal area of Kenya, numbers no more than 300 now and is threatened by hunting for its meat. The rare and little known Jentink's duiker, which occurs in Liberia and the neighboring part of Ivory Coast, and Abbott's duiker, which lives in the high forests of Kilimanjaro and a few neighboring mountains in Tanzania, face similar difficulties. ■

springbok populations, both of which are a tiny fraction of the size they once were. Springbok are still fairly common in remote areas, but they were exterminated by hunters in many others, and the huge numbers previously seen on migration are irrevocably a thing of the past.

FARMING

Springbok were shot, virtually on sight, not just for their meat but more important because they were perceived to be a threat to crops. Damage caused by their mass migrations spurred farmers to shoot the animals whenever they appeared near farmland. Fears of crop-raiding, along with the fear that wild ungulates may compete with livestock for grazing on open pasture, have brought many gazelle species into deadly conflict with farmers. But such fears are often exaggerated, and the irony is that gazelles are often forced into farming areas because they have nowhere else to go.

The ever-increasing use of land for cultivation and livestock pasture in Africa and Asia has steadily reduced the habitat available to support gazelles, dwarf

ANTELOPES IN DANGER

THE FOLLOWING ARE LISTED BY THE IUCN (1994):

JENTINK'S DUIKER	ENDANGERED
CUVIER'S GAZELLE	ENDANGERED
DAMA GAZELLE	ENDANGERED
SLENDER-HORNED GAZELLE	ENDANGERED
ABBOTT'S DUIKER	VULNERABLE
ADER'S DUIKER	VULNERABLE
OGILBY'S DUIKER	VULNERABLE
ZEBRA DUIKER	VULNERABLE
BLACKBUCK	VULNERABLE
DORCAS GAZELLE	VULNERABLE
MOUNTAIN GAZELLE	VULNERABLE
RED-FRONTED GAZELLE	VULNERABLE
SOEMMERRING'S GAZELLE	VULNERABLE
SPEKE'S GAZELLE	VULNERABLE

ENDANGERED MEANS THE SPECIES' SURVIVAL IS UNLIKELY IF THE CAUSAL FACTORS CONTINUE OPERATING. VULNERABLE SPECIES ARE BELIEVED LIKELY TO MOVE INTO THE ENDANGERED CATEGORY IN THE NEAR FUTURE IF CAUSAL FACTORS CONTINUE.

INTO THE FUTURE

Despite the passing of protective laws in most countries, the slow decline of most antelope species is likely to continue. Hunting may have passed its heyday, but poaching still occurs, and the gradual diminution of habitat goes on undiminished.

But the story is not all negative. Measures have been taken to conserve gazelles and their habitats, and many preserves now have thriving populations. The goitered gazelle in Turkestan is a prime example. Once very common, it was hunted so intensely this century that in 1960 a mere 30 survived. But two nature reserves in Badkhyz in Turkmenistan and Shirvan in Azerbaijan proved to be the species' saviors. In 16 years the total population had climbed again to 20,000. The Tibetan gazelle looks secure, not just because its habitat is so remote but because the 95,000-sq-mi (240,000-sq-km) Chang Tang Wildlife Reserve now covers much of its range.

PREDICTION

A PRECARIOUS FUTURE

Without adequate protection from poachers and with few established refuges in places they still inhabit, the future looks grim for the most endangered duikers and gazelles, such as the dama, slender-horned, and Cuvier's gazelles.

In South Africa, springbok are secure since many thousands of them have been reintroduced to reserves and private game ranches. Thriving populations of blackbuck have been established still farther afield. Released on the pampas grasslands in 1906, they are reputed by now to have reached pest proportions in Argentina. Across private ranches in Texas, there are vast herds of blackbuck, and ten of these were reintroduced experimentally into the Lal Suhanra National Park in Pakistan.

The arid southern lands of Arabia are still home to scant herds of mountain gazelles, and since 1991, 30 more have been reintroduced to the Special Ibex Reserve 125 miles (200 kilometers) south of Riyadh in Saudi Arabia. They were raised at the King Khalid Wildlife Research Center, which was set up in the country primarily for research and captive breeding of indigenous gazelles. Already the returnees have produced a dozen fawns in the wild, and there are plans to reintroduce more of these and other species at various sites. ∎

HUMAN CONFLICT

Species that are much reduced in number and restricted in area are always prone to catastrophe, whatever the quality of their refuge. Disease outbreaks from domestic livestock and freak climatic aberrations can rapidly wipe out years of conservation progress.

In parts of Africa and Asia, another grim factor has exacerbated the decline of local species: human conflict. The problem is not just the havoc and destruction that war brings, but also the fact that as firearms become more widespread, as law enforcement breaks down, and as food supplies are disrupted, the poaching of game becomes rife. The dibatag has reputedly been hard hit by warfare in the Horn of Africa (Somalia and Ethiopia), while military conflict in the Golan Heights, in extreme southwest Syria, has centered on just the area where several hundred mountain gazelles were relocated in the 1970s.

More recently, fighting between rebels and the army in 1989 and again since 1992 has effectively halted any protection of the important Basse Casamance National Park in Senegal. People now hunt freely in the reserve, and some animals have disappeared entirely, among them the yellow-backed duiker.

Steve Roberts/Wildlife Art Agency

GIBBONS

RELATIONS

Gibbons belong to the primate order. Other members of this order include:

HUMAN

ORANGUTANS

GORILLAS

CHIMPANZEES

OLD WORLD MONKEYS

NEW WORLD MONKEYS

PROSIMIANS

J. Tinning/Frank Lane Picture Agency

Gibbons are primates, most closely related to the great apes of the family Pongidae. At one time they were placed in a subfamily known as the Hylobatinae, but now they are more usually contained in a family of their own, the Hylobatidae. All nine species of gibbon belong to the same genus.

ORDER
Primates

FAMILY
Hylobatidae

GENUS
Hylobates

SPECIES
*syndactylus
concolor
hoolock
klossii
pileatus
muelleri
moloch
agilis
lar*

SINGING FROM THE TREETOPS

FOUND ONLY IN THE TROPICAL FORESTS OF SOUTHEAST ASIA, THESE MEMBERS OF THE PRIMATE ORDER ARE SMALL, AGILE, AND EXTREMELY ACTIVE. THEY ARE ALSO VERY SHY AND DIFFICULT TO APPROACH

As dawn breaks and daytime sounds start up in the steamy jungles of Southeast Asia, a noise, more penetrating and distinctive than all others, cuts through the humid air. Ringing out from the very top of a tall tree, it is the song of the male gibbon proclaiming his position as king of his territory. Before long, he is joined in chorus by his female, emphasizing her position as his mate. Together, their songs rise in intensity, until the female takes over to bring the duet to a deafening crescendo. Their presence thus established, together with their offspring, who may also have joined in the song, the pair will begin their daily journey around their territory in a seemingly endless quest for ripe fruit.

All of the nine species of gibbons indulge in singing of this type, although not all necessarily in duets of paired males and females. In some cases, such as the largest of all gibbons—the siamang—it appears to be the female that initiates the call, the male joining in with her. In others, it is the females that are responsible for the "great calls" described variously as "a high trill of a tonal purity that no human soprano could ever challenge" and "the finest music uttered by any land mammal."

OLDEST SWINGERS IN TOWN!

Gibbons are apes—members of a family that is usually divided into the great apes, comprising the chimpanzees, orangutans and gorillas, and the lesser apes—the gibbons. Markedly smaller than their perhaps better-known relatives, the gibbons are the consummate tree dwellers, swinging from branch to branch in their jungle habitats with grace and accuracy. They are considered to be the most primitive of the apes, and yet in terms of numbers and distribution they are by far the most successful.

The first indication of gibbonlike ancestors close to their current Southeast Asian range is a gibbon tooth dating from between 10–8 million years ago found in the Siwalik hills of India. More fossils appeared in China from around one million years ago—apparently about the time that they began to spread farther down into southeast Asia. Populations became isolated in three distinct areas—southwest, northeast, and east—and developed into three distinct lineages that subsequently gave rise to the nine species there today.

Gerald Cubitt/Bruce Coleman Ltd.

J. Hobday/Natural Science Photos

Known as the agile gibbon, this species lives up to its name as it swings through the forest canopy (above).

 **SIGHT**

COLOR VARIATION

All gibbons share the same anatomical features and characteristics, as well as environment preferences, dietary requirements, and daily habits. Except for the noticeably larger siamang, all are also much the same size, yet, across their range, they vary quite considerably in coat color. In some species, such as the siamang and kloss gibbons, males and females are the same color across their range; in others, such as the agile and lar gibbons, males and females in one location will share the same coat color, but in another area, the color may be quite different. The male and female of the hoolock gibbon are the same color until the female reaches maturity, at which point her coat lightens considerably. The reason for these variations is uncertain, other than that the different species developed separately in their various locations.

It seems that early primates generally moved about on all fours, as the great apes still do. As they spread out to occupy different ecological niches, they developed characteristics and adaptations that would better suit their particular environment. The gibbons became the most arboreal of all the apes, and because their mode of locomotion through the trees is to swing by their arms, the relative size of their front limbs to their hind limbs increased. All gibbons have elongated arms—the spread of which can be almost twice the length of the body—and also fingers that are designed to wrap around branches like hooks. In fact, relative to the length of the body, the legs are also quite long, but this often gets overlooked because of the extraordinarily long arms. All gibbons are tailless.

Largest of all the gibbons is the siamang, *Hylobates syndactylus*, the head-and-body length of which may be up to 3 ft (90 cm) and whose arm spread can be as much as 5 ft (1.5 m). This large black gibbon shares its range in the north with one of the best known of all species, the common white-handed or lar gibbon, *H. lar* (see Fact File, page 789), which is much smaller, weighing only half as much as the siamang. In the southern part of the range, the siamang overlaps with another species, the agile gibbon, *H. agilis*. This gibbon is

Müller's gibbon with its distinctive white eyebrows.

Its coat varies from mouse gray to brown.

about the same size as the lar and also varies in color in different parts of its location, from a golden buff, often with an almost red tinge, through shades of brown to black. Both sexes have the same coat color; males have white eyebrows and cheeks, whereas females have white eyebrows only.

Approximately the same size as the lar and agile gibbons, the kloss gibbon, *H. klossii*, is one that has an overall glossy black coat in which the fur is considerably less dense than in the siamang and the lar. Because of its black color, it is sometimes called the dwarf siamang. It is particularly noted for its song, although it is one of the species in which the male and female sing separately rather than give a duet.

Slightly larger is the hoolock gibbon, *H. hoolock*. In this species the male is black, as is the female until she reaches maturity at about seven years old when her coat turns a golden buff color, which is palest on the top of the head. Both sexes have white eyebrows. The male of the white-cheeked or concolor gibbon, *H. concolor*, is black with grayish or reddish hairs on his cheeks and chin. The female begins life with black fur, but also changes to a golden buff.

Males of the pileated gibbon, *H. pileatus*, are black with white or grayish hair on the temples and on the hands and feet. The females are silvery gray or buff colored with black hair around the face and on the chest. Müller's gibbon, *H. muelleri*, is another whose coat color varies but is typically a mousy gray or brown. The female has markedly darker

---

THE UPSTANDING TUFT OF HAIR ON THE CONCOLOR GIBBON'S HEAD HAS EARNED IT AN ALIAS—THE CRESTED GIBBON

---

hairs on the top of her head and chest, and both sexes have white eyebrows. The moloch gibbon, *H. moloch*, occasionally called the silvery gibbon, has, as this name suggests, a silvery, blue-gray coat with a darker chest and crown of the head.

"SINGING SAC"

To emphasize their song, many gibbons have an inflatable air sac just beneath their throat. This is largest and most noticeable in the siamang and is possessed by both sexes. It is hairless, gray or pinkish gray, and can be puffed up like a large balloon when the gibbons are singing, giving an even greater booming resonance to the song. The siamang's song is said to be a scream, or shriek, from the male and a series of harsh barks from the female. The hoolock is another with such a sac, although this is much smaller than that of the siamang. ∎

Color illustrations Steve Kingston

THE GIBBONS' FAMILY TREE

The primate order is divided into two main types: the lower primates or prosimians, which include lemurs, galagos, lorises, pottos, and tarsiers; and the higher primates, which include monkeys, apes, and also humans. The chimpanzees, orangutans, and gorillas are grouped together as the great apes, while the nine species of gibbons are known as the lesser apes.

SIAMANG
Hylobates syndactylus
(HIE-loe-bay-tees sin-DACK-till-us)

The largest of all the gibbons, the siamang is occasionally placed in the subgenus Symphalangus. It has the longest fur of any species and, unlike all other gibbons, it has a webbing-type membrane between the second and third toes of its feet. The large air sac that lies beneath the chin in both sexes apparently gives the song two distinctly different notes, one a low boom and the other a high-pitched bark.

NEW WORLD
MONKEYS

OLD WORLD
MONKEYS

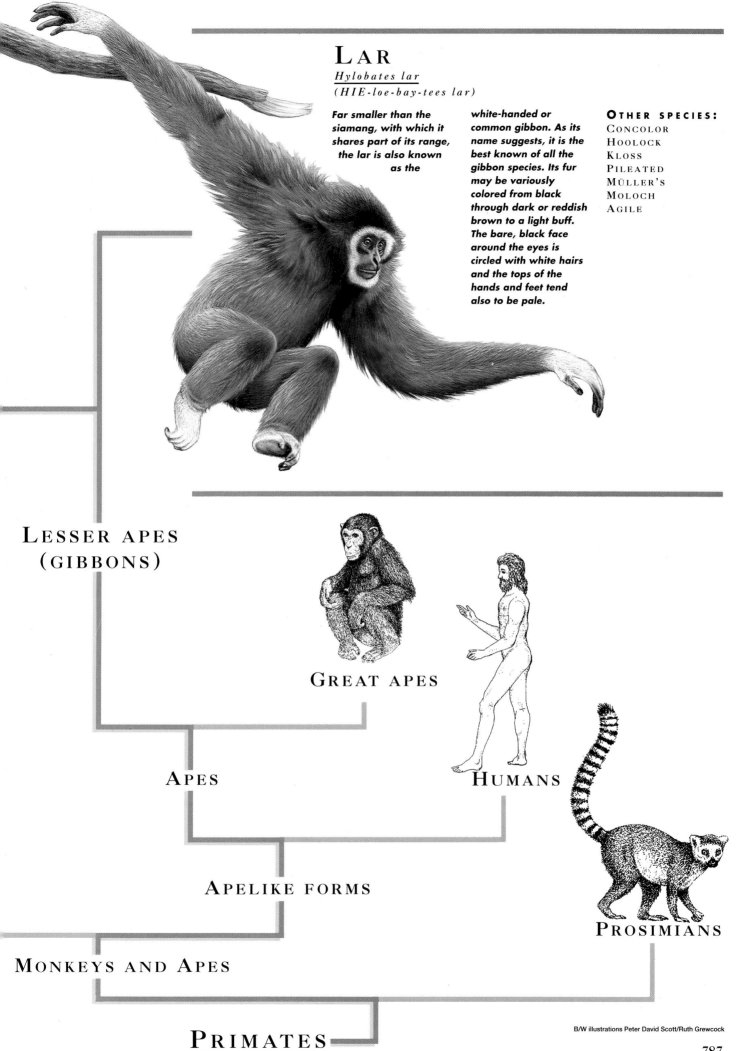

LAR

Hylobates lar
(*HIE-loe-bay-tees lar*)

Far smaller than the siamang, with which it shares part of its range, the lar is also known as the white-handed or common gibbon. As its name suggests, it is the best known of all the gibbon species. Its fur may be variously colored from black through dark or reddish brown to a light buff. The bare, black face around the eyes is circled with white hairs and the tops of the hands and feet tend also to be pale.

OTHER SPECIES:
CONCOLOR
HOOLOCK
KLOSS
PILEATED
MÜLLER'S
MOLOCH
AGILE

LESSER APES
(GIBBONS)

GREAT APES

APES

HUMANS

APELIKE FORMS

PROSIMIANS

MONKEYS AND APES

PRIMATES

B/W illustrations Peter David Scott/Ruth Grewcock

787

ANATOMY:
THE GIBBON

X-ray illustrations Elisabeth Smith

HANDS & FEET
The long fingers of the hand (right) hook over the branches. The deeply cleft feet (far right) help the gibbon walk upright.

The siamang (above left) has a head-and-body length of some 3 ft (90 cm) and can weigh up to 28.5 lb (13 kg). The other species, including the lar (above right), are approximately half this size.

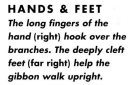

THE ARMS

are extremely long with highly mobile joints that help to propel the gibbon through the trees. Swinging from branch to branch is the the gibbon's specialty.

X RAY

Despite the fact that on the ground the gibbon moves on its hind feet in a similar manner to humans, its skeleton is nowhere near as erect. The pelvis is lengthened to allow for muscle attachment that helps it stand erect when necessary. The scapulae (shoulder blades) are situated on the back of the thorax, as in humans, but this placement differs from that in the Old World monkeys.

GIBBON SKULL

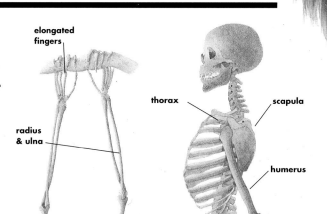

elongated fingers

radius & ulna

humerus

scapula

thorax

elongated pelvis

thorax

scapula

humerus

radius & ulna

pelvis

canines

shallow lower jaw

THE SKULL
The skulls of gibbons differ from the great apes in having a much shallower lower jaw. Where the skulls of other apes show a considerable difference in size between males and females, this is not so among gibbons. Equally, the canine teeth are virtually the same size in both sexes.

ARMS AND SHOULDERS
With its extremely long arms and hooklike hands, the gibbon is the best adapted ape to move by brachiation—swinging from branch to branch by the arms. The shoulder joints are extremely mobile and possess very strong muscles.

THE LEGS

are long, although considerably shorter than the arms. The feet are also smaller than the hands. Gibbons are the only apes to stand upright and walk on their hind feet on the ground, their stance being plantigrade, that is, walking first on the heels then soles of the feet.

GIBBON SKELETON

HUMAN SKELETON

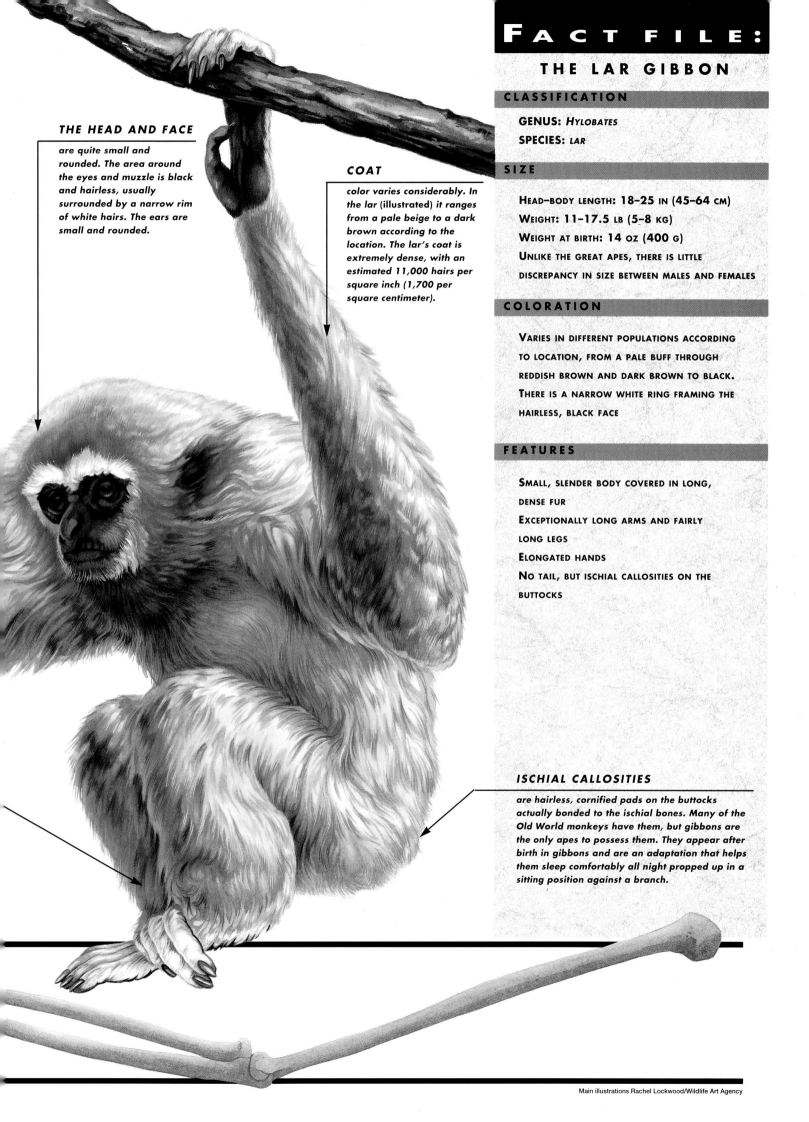

THE HEAD AND FACE

are quite small and rounded. The area around the eyes and muzzle is black and hairless, usually surrounded by a narrow rim of white hairs. The ears are small and rounded.

COAT

color varies considerably. In the lar (illustrated) it ranges from a pale beige to a dark brown according to the location. The lar's coat is extremely dense, with an estimated 11,000 hairs per square inch (1,700 per square centimeter).

FACT FILE:

THE LAR GIBBON

CLASSIFICATION

GENUS: *HYLOBATES*
SPECIES: *LAR*

SIZE

HEAD–BODY LENGTH: 18–25 IN (45–64 CM)
WEIGHT: 11–17.5 LB (5–8 KG)
WEIGHT AT BIRTH: 14 OZ (400 G)
UNLIKE THE GREAT APES, THERE IS LITTLE DISCREPANCY IN SIZE BETWEEN MALES AND FEMALES

COLORATION

VARIES IN DIFFERENT POPULATIONS ACCORDING TO LOCATION, FROM A PALE BUFF THROUGH REDDISH BROWN AND DARK BROWN TO BLACK. THERE IS A NARROW WHITE RING FRAMING THE HAIRLESS, BLACK FACE

FEATURES

SMALL, SLENDER BODY COVERED IN LONG, DENSE FUR
EXCEPTIONALLY LONG ARMS AND FAIRLY LONG LEGS
ELONGATED HANDS
NO TAIL, BUT ISCHIAL CALLOSITIES ON THE BUTTOCKS

ISCHIAL CALLOSITIES

are hairless, cornified pads on the buttocks actually bonded to the ischial bones. Many of the Old World monkeys have them, but gibbons are the only apes to possess them. They appear after birth in gibbons and are an adaptation that helps them sleep comfortably all night propped up in a sitting position against a branch.

Main illustrations Rachel Lockwood/Wildlife Art Agency

CARTWHEELS IN THE AIR

GIBBONS LIVE IN TIGHTLY KNIT FAMILY GROUPS IN CLEARLY DEMARCATED AND DEFENDED TERRITORIES. THEY ARE THE CONSUMMATE ACROBATS OF THE TROPICAL FOREST'S HIGH CANOPY

Active during the day, gibbons are among the most restless of all primates, spending their time traveling around their territories looking for the ripe fruit of which they are so fond. Their hunger temporarily assuaged, they may sit back in the fork of a branch, sunning themselves for a while, or drape themselves across a branch while a close relative indulges in attentive social grooming. For the rest of the time, they move more quickly, more quietly, and farther around the forest each day than any other forest ape or monkey. It is thought that they can move through the forest at speeds in excess of 20 mph (32 km/h).

TREE-DWELLING ACROBATS

Gibbons are the most complete tree dwellers of all the apes. Their genus name, *Hylobates*, means "dweller in the trees" or "tree traveler," and although their relatives the chimpanzees also swing through the trees, gibbons are undoubtedly the most efficient, and some say the only true, brachiators. In this form of locomotion, the animal does not leap from branch to branch, but instead almost cartwheels along beneath the branches, using its arms alternately in a swinging movement that propels it through the air and across gaps of 29.5 ft (9 m) or more.

All the propulsion for the leap comes from the shoulders and arms; gibbons do not jump from branch to branch by pushing off with their hind legs as some monkeys do. Equally, the hands do not grasp the branches, as this would slow the movement; instead, they simply hook over them so that they can be quickly released for the next swing that will take the gibbon to a higher or lower branch with equal ease. During each swing, the body acts like a pendulum, pivoting through a 180-degree rotation. So mobile are the shoulder and elbow joints that a gibbon can hang from a branch and slowly rotate its

body through almost 360 degrees. Its slender form—it is by far the smallest and lightest of the apes—means it can suspend itself by one arm from the apparently fragile end of the thinnest of branches while picking fruit with the free hand. Gibbons have excellent binocular vision, which enables them to focus quickly and accurately on the branches ahead.

The hands have become efficient hooks at the expense of dexterity. In order to grip objects

Wardene Weisser/Ardea

Water is a natural boundary for gibbons and effectively keeps species apart (above).

Morten Strange/NHPA

between finger and thumb, the end pad of each must be able to come into close, firm contact. Because the thumb in the gibbon is shortened and branches out almost from the gibbon's wrist, it is not able to achieve this contact. Without this precision grip, if a gibbon wants to pick something up from off a branch, it generally does so by cupping its fingers and sweeping up the object in the palm of its hand in a sideways movement.

On the ground and along branches that are too thick for the fingers to hook over, gibbons walk in a plantigrade stance, like humans—the only ape to do this. The great apes will occasionally take a few steps forward on their hind legs, but the gait tends to be slow and clumsy. This is not the case in the gibbons, which walk with ease on their hind legs, although they generally hold their long arms out at shoulder height to help them balance and also to get them out of the way.

ALTHOUGH THEY FORAGE ALONE, FAMILIES MAY COME TOGETHER TO REST, GROOM, AND SLEEP AT NIGHT

Night is the time for sleeping, and this is accomplished propped up against a branch high in a tall tree, well hidden among the leaves. Unlike some other apes, gibbons do not make any sort of treetop nest, but simply curl themselves up tightly in their sitting position, resting on the ischial callosities— the horny, hairless pads on their buttocks. Usually they pull their knees up to their chests, bury their heads between the knees and chest, and wrap their long arms around themselves.

With no inner coat of fine hair to act as insulation, gibbons present as little surface as possible to the elements, thereby keeping as dry and as warm as possible. This is particularly important, for they tend to sleep high up in tall trees, choosing those that are sufficiently robust to remain steady in the strong winds of the forest. Although they are thus exposed to the rain when it falls, it does mean they do not spend the rest of the night being dripped upon from the leaves and branches above them; occasionally they shake themselves vigorously, like a wet dog, to dispel the rain from their fur.

This position near the top of the tree is also important for their early morning song, which they want to be heard around the forest; farther down the tree the thick canopy of branches and leaves would act as a sound muffler, reducing the effect of the concert. ∎

Gibbons spend much of their time simply "hanging around" their forest home.

HABITATS

Jean-Paul Ferrero/Ardea

Sitting comfortably in its treetop home, the Müller's gibbon (left) is found only in Borneo. The home range of a family group covers about 75–100 acres (30–40 ha), of which 90 percent is defended against neighboring groups.

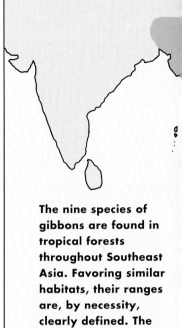

The nine species of gibbons are found in tropical forests throughout Southeast Asia. Favoring similar habitats, their ranges are, by necessity, clearly defined. The occasional overlap tends to be separated by water—which gibbons will not cross.

All nine species of gibbons are found in the same type of habitat—the equatorial or tropical rain forests of the Indo-Malayan subregion. The forests that these gibbons share with orangutans, tarsiers, tree shrews, tapirs, and flying lemurs have covered the area since the Pliocene era, which began five million years ago, and the trees range from sea level up to altitudes of at least 9,850 ft (3,000 m). Gibbons seem to favor the lowland and hilly forests, although the siamang may be found in the submontane forests up to about 5,900 ft (1,800 m); the lar gibbon has been observed higher still.

EVERYTHING FOR THE HOME

The forests obviously provide gibbons with all that they need—tall trees that provide them with shelter, somewhere to rest and sleep, and also food. Because the ecological requirements of all gibbon species are so similar, it would be virtually impossible for them to coexist in the same area, and in consequence there is very little overlap between species.

Although different species may appear to inhabit the same area, they are usually separated by rivers, which gibbons will not cross. The notable difference to this occurs in the siamang, which is found in the Malay Peninsula and Sumatra. In the northern part of its range, it overlaps to some extent with the best known of all gibbons, the lar, which occurs from the Burma-Yunnan border south to parts of Thailand and the Malay Peninsula and northern Sumatra. In the southern part of its range, it shares its habitat with the agile gibbon, which also occurs in parts of

FOCUS ON

THE SUMATRAN RAIN FOREST

The island of Sumatra is one of the Great Sunda Islands and the second largest island of the Indonesia archipelago after Borneo. The equator crosses it, dividing it almost exactly into two. It is approximately 1,069 miles (1,722 km) long and 324 miles (520 km) across at its widest point. There is a high mountain chain that runs along the western coast, the highest peak of which is 12,483 ft (3,805 m). The forests begin at some 300–400 ft (90–120 m) above sea level and continue to all but the very highest mountain peaks, providing a number of different vegetation zones according to altitude. The island's animal life is concentrated in the forests and is similar to that of Borneo, rather than to that of the closer island of Java. Besides siamang, lar, and agile gibbons, it includes the banded leaf monkey, the silvered leaf monkey, and the pig-tailed and crab-eating macaques, as well as bats, flying squirrels, the wild dog, wild boar, and civet cat.

Morten Strange/NHPA

DISTRIBUTION

KEY

SIAMANG GIBBON

KLOSS GIBBON

HOOLOCK GIBBON

CONCOLOR GIBBON

LAR GIBBON

PILEATED GIBBON

MÜLLER'S GIBBON

MOLOCH GIBBON

AGILE GIBBON

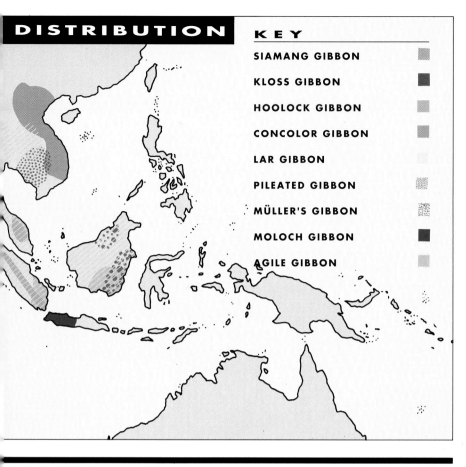

the Malay Peninsula, southwestern Borneo, and much of Sumatra except the north.

The siamang's larger size means it needs more food each day than the other gibbons. However, it tends to travel less far around the forest each day than other species and therefore has to be less selective about its food, concentrating its efforts in a few heavy-fruiting trees and supplementing its diet with quite a large quantity of leaves.

The agile and lar gibbons will range over a much wider area to feed, finding much of their food at the smaller, more widely dispersed trees that the siamangs do not visit. They may also be found higher up in the trees, often in the forest's upper story or canopy at heights of 118–148 ft (36–45 m); siamangs, it seems, are usually found in the upper ranges of the middle story at heights of no more than 82–98 ft (25–30 m) above the ground.

The lar's northern Thailand range makes it the most northerly dwelling of the species. To the west of it, the hoolock gibbon occurs, its range covering Assam, Myanmar, and Bangladesh, while to the east is found the concolor gibbon, whose range covers Laos, Vietnam, Hainan, southeastern China, and eastern Cambodia. The pileated gibbon is found farther south and to the east in Thailand, ranging also into Cambodia. Northeastern Borneo is home to Müller's gibbon, the agile gibbon dwelling mainly in the southwest of this large island. The kloss gibbon occurs in western Sumatra, although it is found mainly in the Mentawai Islands, which lie to the west of Sumatra itself. The moloch gibbon is the sole gibbon inhabitant of western Java. ∎

KEY FACTS

● In a typical 123 acres (50 hectares) of rain forest in the Malay Peninsula, there are more species of trees than there are in the whole of North America.

● Tropical rain forests cover only about 7 percent of the earth's land surface, yet they contain more than half of its tree species and 60 percent of plant species. They are also home to 80 percent of all insect species and 90 percent of all primate species.

● Probably as many as two-thirds of the animal and insect species that live in tropical rain forests spend their entire lives in the trees, never venturing to the ground.

FOOD AND FEEDING

For all gibbons, fruit is the mainstay of their diet, and unlike some of the monkeys that feed in the same trees, gibbons mainly seek out fruit that is really ripe. As they may find only a few in any given tree, they are constantly traveling onward. Some 35 percent of the ten hours or so of the active day is spent in actual feeding, and almost as much time is spent traveling from tree to tree.

RIPE FOR THE PICKING

Favorite fruits are pulpy ones, figs in particular, but also mangoes and a fruit called latso. Figs are a particular favorite because, it seems, they can be plucked in handfuls and eaten whole. Often a gibbon will pause on a branch and gently squeeze

years—or even longer. There is no evidence to suggest that gibbons store knowledge of when trees are likely to fruit. Instead, it seems, they find out only by traveling around and testing, and they may watch and follow flocks of fruit-eating hornbills and pigeons—some of their principal competitors for fruit at the levels they frequent. It also seems that gibbons mainly concentrate their feeding on three or four species of trees at a time.

Fruit is rich in carbohydrate, but quite low in protein—a deficiency that must be made good in some way. To do so, gibbons eat a certain amount of leaves, as well as other vegetable matter such as buds and flowers. The tips of vines seem to be a favorite, broken off and chewed down like an

Patrick Fagot/NHPA

A gibbon drinks from its cupped hand. This is as near to water as this wary gibbon is prepared to go.

a fruit between the thumb and the side of the index finger. It is thought unlikely that the gibbon is testing for ripeness, which is generally indicated in these fruits by color, and gibbons can see color. Instead, it has been suggested that the effect of the squeezing could be to make the fruits ripen faster, so the gibbon will know it can soon visit that tree again.

This could well be an important factor to a group of gibbons. There are sometimes as many as 250 species of fruiting trees in any given home range, and unlike trees in more temperate regions, they do not bear ripe fruit with seasonal regularity. Some bear fruit almost continually or at least every few months; some produce a crop just once a year; while others may bear fruit only once every ten

PICKING INSECTS
From time to time a gibbon will venture down from its treetop home to search for grubs and insects on the forest floor.

Illustration Peter David Scott/Wildlife Art Agency

asparagus stem, until they become too tough. Gibbons also eat insects, birds' and geckos' eggs, as well as small lizards and spiders and occasionally even birds, if they can catch them. Often gibbons will sit on a branch of a tree that has flaking bark and carefully strip it away to search for insect larvae underneath. At other times, they may grab a handful of moss, lichen, and small twigs and search through this to see if it contains any insects.

FAST WORKERS

Almost all activity in a gibbon's daily life is speedy, and gathering fruit and eating are no exceptions. A gibbon moves quickly around a tree, picking ripe fruits, never sitting in one place for long. Often it will hang suspended from a light branch with one hand, the other being used to quickly pluck ripe figs off the tree, popping them into a mouth that is still full from the previous intake. In palm trees, a gibbon will often walk along the long, stout leaves, its arms held outward to balance, to get to the 2-ft- (60-cm-) long bunches of fruit. This it hangs on to with its hands, extracting one of the tennis-ball-sized fruits with its teeth.

Fruit is usually swallowed seeds and all, but fibrous rind or peel will first be stripped off with the long canines possessed by all apes. The molars have a feature shared by other apes and humans—a prominent crest running across the tooth. This aids in grinding fibrous vegetation and in apes is associated with powerful chewing muscles. Although the digestive system is comparatively simple, the cecum and colon in the gibbon are somewhat enlarged to enable it to cope with the fibrous nature of leaves while extracting their protein content. ■

in SIGHT

WARY OF WATER

By and large, gibbons are animals that eschew water as much as possible, apparently being afraid of it; as they rarely descend to the ground, they seldom come into contact with it and they certainly are not natural or happy swimmers.

They obtain their necessary liquid requirements either from the fruit they eat, from dew or rain on leaves, or by dipping their fingers, hands, and sometimes arms into reservoirs of rainwater in tree hollows or "cups" formed by plants and then sucking their fur to get the liquid. They may also lift water to their lips in their cupped hands.

EATING GREENS

Gibbons will eat leaves, buds, and flowers for extra protein. And for the bulky siamang, this amounts to more than half its total diet.

FISTFUL OF FRUIT

Hanging from a branch with one hand, a gibbon uses its other hand to provide a favorite "fast-food" meal of fruit.

SOCIAL STRUCTURE

Gibbons display one of the tightest, most strongly bonded family structures of any in the mammal kingdom. A family unit consists of a mated male and female and up to four of their offspring at any given time. Such a group may stay stable for five or six years, being finally disrupted by the arrival of a new baby, by the dominant male's intolerance of a subordinate male, or by the beginnings of that male's urge to mate.

Each family group has a very clearly defined home range, about 75 percent of which could be termed its territory—this being the area that the group, the dominant male in particular, defends vigorously. Home ranges of different groups will be extensively adjacent, but the overlap is usually remarkably small. Challenges and physical encounters between dominant males may occur in the overlapping area, or they may occur in the no-man's-land between the two territories.

The home range of a gibbon group varies from 40–300 acres (16–121 hectares), but the average size is some 84 acres (34 hectares), of which 62 acres (25 hectares) will be defended.

Siamangs, although the largest of the species, tend to have the smallest home ranges—sometimes only half the size of their smaller relatives'. Siamangs rarely travel more than 0.6 mile (1 km) in a day and usually feed at no more than eight feeding sites. Other species may travel up to twice this distance and feed at twice as many sites, although far less thoroughly at each one. It has been estimated that gibbons in the forests of Malaysia consistently travel twice as far around the forest each day as any other tree-living primate.

THE LAY OF THE LAND

It is likely that this tight-knit family group-structure has come about as a result of the somewhat small, scattered food sources in the jungle. Although there are thousands of trees within a group's home range, gibbons generally concentrate their feeding on only three or four species at a time, the fruiting seasons ranging in duration from just a few days to several months. In order to insure an adequate supply of food, it is best to live within a fixed area, the geography and contents of which can be thoroughly learned. The home range of gibbons is among the smallest of all primate species, thereby enabling them to grasp thoroughly with the contours and the indigenous trees.

Lar gibbons grooming each other. Social grooming is an important part of gibbon family life.

COLOR CODED
The color of a gibbon's coat may vary according to species, location, sex, and age. This family group of hoolock gibbons shows the black male, golden female, and whitish infant.

Alain Compost/Bruce Coleman Ltd.

In most species, the gibbons' day starts at about six in the morning when the group leaves its sleeping tree and takes off through the forest to a feeding tree. It seems that, in some species at least, the family engages in an early-morning major feeding bout for about one hour before they begin their calls *(see page 798)*. Sleeping quarters tend to be fairly central in a home range, so movement away from these trees will soon bring them close to one of the boundaries. A gibbon group will generally visit at least one area of its territory boundaries during the course of a day.

SETTLING DISPUTES

Should either their calls or a boundary visit bring about a territorial dispute with another group, it is the dominant male that will offer or accept a challenge. This usually begins with a characteristic vocalization from the male, sometimes described as a "conflict-hoo"; in the lar gibbon it is a medium-to-loud noise emitted in a rapid series over a period of two to three seconds, getting ever louder. While calling, a male may also give an energetic display in which he hangs by one arm from a branch, twisting this way and that, before swinging noisily around a small circular or oval area. He may break off dead branches from trees and hurl them to the forest floor, thereby increasing the noise, and thus the display of aggression. If the intruder is not deterred, a chase may ensue, followed by an actual fight in which males attempt to force their opponent out of the trees by pushing or kicking them or actually dropping on them from a higher branch. Damage is also inflicted with the teeth.

Often while such an encounter is going on, the female of the group, together with her offspring,

---

OLDER MALE GIBBONS OFTEN HAVE TORN EARS AND DISPLAY BATTLE SCARS ON THEIR FACES

---

will calmly continue feeding. This means that the dominant male's feeding time is often reduced, and it may be that he feeds later in the middle of the day or evening to make up for this.

Generally the group will rest in the hottest hours of the day, lazing back against a branch or indulging in social grooming. An hour or two later, they are off again searching for food until about 4:30 in the afternoon, when they return to the tree or trees selected for sleeping that night. Usually members of a family group will sleep a few yards apart from one another, each one choosing a robust, horizontal branch on which to curl up and sleep; occasionally they may share sleeping quarters. ∎

in SIGHT

SOCIAL GROOMING

Bonds within a family group of gibbons are constantly reinforced by the act of social grooming, which may be done by any two members. As the group stops to rest in the middle of the day, one gibbon will drape him- or herself over a branch to have its fur and skin minutely examined and picked over by another.

Often the female and one or another of her young will do this while the male is proclaiming his morning song. The one being groomed constantly shifts position so that every part of its body can be reached. The process may go on for some time, until, by mutual consent, the two change roles.

Illustration Kim Thompson

SONGS

The loud calls or songs uttered by all gibbons are among the most amazing of all noises to come from the animal kingdom. Although in all species they perform the same function—that of developing and maintaining a pair bond, advertising a group's presence and a territory—the vocalizations themselves are different in each species. The hoolock gibbon, for example, takes its name from the sound of the call it makes.

Loud noises among primates tend to be most developed in those species that, by their diet and anatomy, are restricted to habitats with the densest vegetation and poorest visibility. Gibbons have evolved to some extent to fill the ecological niche of gathering food by hanging from the merest twig or the extreme end of a slender branch. If they were any bigger, they would not be able to exploit this niche. Their small size is therefore essential to their survival, on the one hand, but, on the other, it could prove a disadvantage in the defense of their territory against intruders. To compensate, a male shows his confidence and aptitude in this regard by "singing" loudly and for a long time, usually quite close to a territory boundary. Clearly there is an association between the noise and territorial defense, for males will howl particularly loudly during face-to-face encounters, before and between treetop chases, and while indulging in acrobatic or branch- and leaf-tearing displays, all designed to scare off an intruder.

MORNING CHORUS

In some species of gibbons, the male begins the song, and usually starts quite early in the morning, having first climbed high into the canopy of a tall tree. Before long the female, and possibly also her young, join him in what can become an elaborate duet. Each sings his or her own individual song, the two combining together intricately and doubtless serving to reinforce the bond between the mated pair. In other species, it is the female that takes the lead in this duet, and, indeed, it is often the females that are attributed with having the "great calls," described as a loud, shrill, wailing crescendo that fills the forest.

As a group gives its morning calls, it stimulates others to do the same. As two groups hear one another, they will often move closer, as if to establish beyond all doubt the boundaries of each territory. They may even change the direction in which they were bound in response to the call of a neighboring group.

Males and females of the lar, agile, moloch,

Color illustration by Steve Kingston

MORNING SONG

Male and female kloss gibbons sing separately. The song of the female has been described as "the finest music uttered by any land mammal."

Dieter & Mary Plage/Survival Anglia Ltd.

Siamangs (above) *sing less often than other gibbons, but, when they do, their call is the loudest of all.*

Müller's, and concolor gibbons all sing in duet, almost every day and generally for an average of about fifteen minutes each day. Sometimes the song, or a version of it, is repeated more than once a day. Males and females of the hoolock and pileated gibbons and the siamang sing at the same time but in the same sort of duet.

The call of the kloss gibbon, particularly that of the female, is said to be the most spectacular of all. The female's "great call" has been described as a "long series of slowly ascending pure notes leading into a bubbling trill." Uniquely, the male and female sing separately. The male generally begins his call around dawn, warming up with some simple whistles before going on to more elaborate trills of varying notes. The song has been known to go on for two hours. ∎

THE SONG OF THE SIAMANG

B/W illustration Ruth Grewcock

The siamang's song is the loudest, and possibly the harshest, of all gibbons. Both sexes possess a large air sac beneath the chin that can be inflated during the call and accounts for the harshness as well as a booming hollow resonance. It seems that the siamang generally starts its song later than the agile and lar gibbons with which it shares its territory; in this way they do not obliterate one another and may more easily hear the others' proclamation. The siamang also calls on average only every three days and rarely more than once a day—significantly less than its smaller relatives. This could be because its larger size causes it to use more energy in traveling around its territory, and it must therefore conserve it where it can and not expend it on unnecessary singing.

LIFE CYCLE

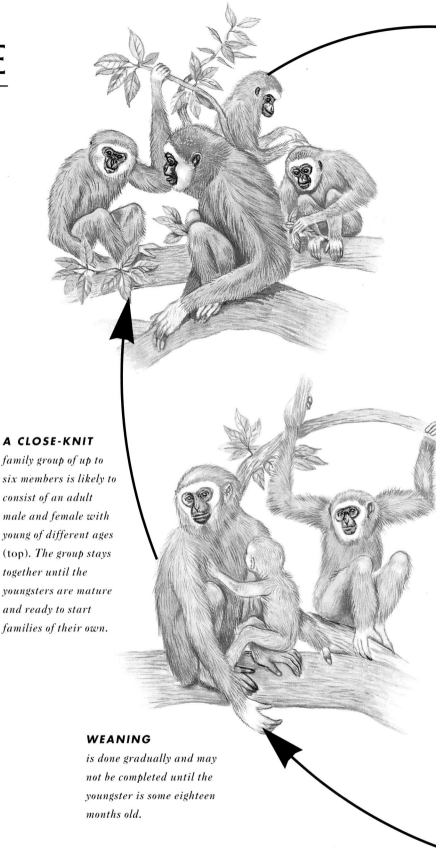

Gibbons are unique among apes in being monogamous—that is in choosing a partner and then pairing with it for life. Such a system suits the gibbons' lifestyle and gives them the highest chance of survival as a species. If mating and bonding were more casual—the family group not so tightly-knit as a result—establishment of territories and thus the most efficient use of forest resources would be far harder to accomplish.

Remarkably little is known about the reproduction of gibbons in the wild. It seems that siamangs give birth from November to March, but the estrous cycle in gibbons corresponds to humans—that is they have a menstrual cycle that lasts twenty-eight days, during which they are able to conceive for about seven days.

LIFE BEGINS

Just one young is born after a gestation period of between 210 and 235 days. A single young will have a better chance of survival than, for example, twins, for from the moment of its birth—high up in the trees—it has to be able to hang tightly on to its mother's fur, with no extra support from her, as she flies through the trees daily to forage. The baby is therefore fully developed and precocious at birth,

The young concolor gibbon's whitish coat (below) *will darken to golden or black depending on its sex.*

Rod Williams/Bruce Coleman Ltd.

A CLOSE-KNIT *family group of up to six members is likely to consist of an adult male and female with young of different ages* (top). *The group stays together until the youngsters are mature and ready to start families of their own.*

WEANING *is done gradually and may not be completed until the youngster is some eighteen months old.*

GROWING UP

The life of a young lar gibbon

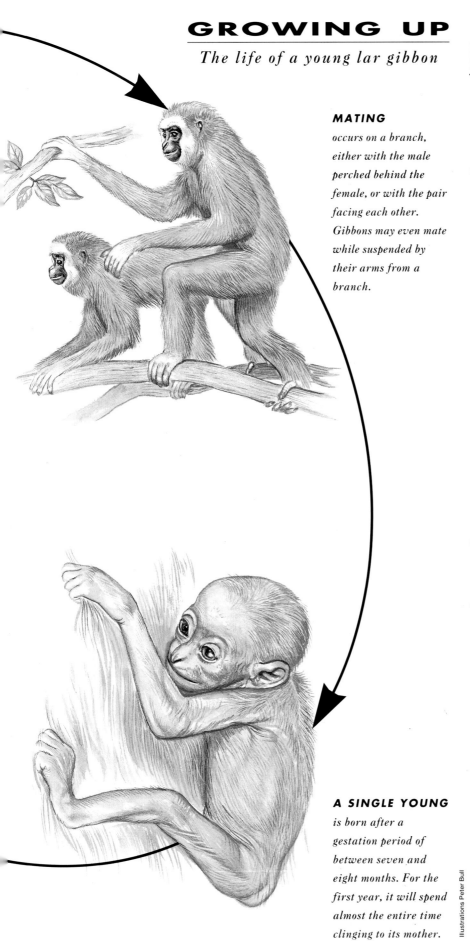

MATING

occurs on a branch, either with the male perched behind the female, or with the pair facing each other. Gibbons may even mate while suspended by their arms from a branch.

A SINGLE YOUNG

is born after a gestation period of between seven and eight months. For the first year, it will spend almost the entire time clinging to its mother.

Illustrations Peter Bull

although it is generally almost naked except for a cap of hair on the crown. When the mother is resting or is still on a branch, the baby will nestle into the fur on her abdomen and thighs in order to keep warm.

The infant grows up close to its parents and will remain in the group probably until it is at least six years old, by which time it will have at least one, probably two, younger siblings. Female gibbons give birth only once every two or three years, again so that attention and care can be focused on the youngest member to give it the best chance of survival. However, because of this and also the territoriality that excludes meeting with other groups, young gibbons do not interact or indulge in play-learning with their peers. While their older siblings may interact with them in a friendly way, most of their interaction is with their parents.

The young gibbon is usually weaned at about 18 months or so. However, by this time, it is usually the father that has taken over daily care of the youngster, particularly in the siamang. The young will

OF ALL THE APES, GIBBON MALES ARE THE ONLY ONES TO FULFILL A CLEAR PARENTAL ROLE

cling to the male's fur as he sets off in search of food, and from him it will learn how to swing through the trees and find the ripest fruit, and how to behave within the family group. Only at night does the father return the youngster to the mother's care.

The group remains tightly knit as the youngsters grow up. They cannot begin to fend for themselves until they are three to four years old, but, by about six years old, the young gibbons will begin to reach puberty. They will begin to interact with the male in both an aggressive and friendly manner and increasingly they have less and less to do with the female, so as not to come into conflict with the dominant male. Eventually, when they are about eight years old, young males begin to occupy the solitary space of no-man's-land between territories, where they begin to sing in the hope of attracting a mate. Solitary or subadult females do not sing; they wait to be wooed by a young male, after which they will establish their own territory and begin a family group. ∎

NOWHERE TO LIVE

ALTHOUGH CONSIDERED THE MOST SUCCESSFUL OF THE APES, THE SPREAD OF GIBBONS HAS REDUCED DRASTICALLY IN RECENT DECADES AND THE FUTURE OF ALL SPECIES APPEARS TO BE UNDER THREAT

P rimates, apes in particular, are humans' closest relative in the animal kingdom, and yet we have done as much to endanger the future of these animals as we have of many others. It was estimated at the beginning of the 1990s that approximately one-third of all primate species or subspecies were in danger of extinction as a direct result of human activities. If extinction does not loom directly, the future of many more is seriously threatened.

TRADE AND TROPHIES
Killed for food, sport, and souvenirs, primates have been meeting their doom at the hands of humans for a long time. The tourist trade has been a rich and demanding one. At one time the capture of primates for live animal trade was also a problem.

Certainly gibbons have been hunted in the wild for food and also to supply a research trade, but these have not significantly affected their numbers. Instead, the principal reason for the demise of the gibbons is that of habitat destruction—the systematic and relentless cutting down and clearing of the tropical forests that are the only environment in which these primates can possibly flourish.

VICTIMS OF COMMERCE
The tropical forests have been cleared in huge tracts in recent times for numbers of reasons. One is for logging—that is, the felling of trees for the commercial use of timber.

A large percentage of any tropical forest is made up of hardwoods, for which worldwide demand has increased hugely in the past fifty years. Most of the woodwork in our houses is hardwood, imported from the tropics. Developed countries apparently import sixteen times more hardwood than they did

in the 1950s. The inevitable result of this is that the export of tropical timber has become one of the five most valuable exports from the developing countries, and, given the amount of indigenous poverty, it would be very difficult for the powers-that-be to

Rod Williams/Bruce Coleman Ltd.

A young male pileated gibbon (above) *in Thailand, where vast areas of rain forest have been destroyed.*

Dr. Ivan Polunin/NHPA

Logging is big business in Southeast Asia. This loss of habitat is threatening the future of gibbons.

THEN & NOW

This map gives an approximate indication of the amount of rain forest that has been destroyed or degraded over the last forty years.

■ **LATE 1980s** ▨ **C. 1940**

Over 40 percent of the world's rain forests have already been destroyed, and much of this deforestation has taken place in India (where almost all primary rain forest has been taken) and throughout all of Southeast Asia, home to the nine species of gibbons. The main causes of this widespread destruction have been logging, agriculture, and, in Cambodia, Vietnam, and Laos, the devastating effects of war.

turn their backs on the demand.

Although in the process of logging only between 4 and 10 percent of trees are actually felled—most of the exports come from only 10 or 12 species out of the more than 600 species in Southeast Asia's forests—it is estimated that in so doing at least 30 percent of the forest is destroyed. The wanted trees may be sited far apart in a tract of forest; necessarily as they are cut down they damage others as they fall, weakening them to such an extent they die anyway or are killed by disease. Clinging vines and other forms of vegetation are also lost in the process, more light and sunshine begins to penetrate the forest, and the balance of the sensitive ecosystem begins to change.

In addition, roads are cut into the forests both

to reach the required trees and then to facilitate the removal of the timber. This increasingly allows ease of access into the once near-impenetrable forest by people to hunt and collect, or simply to observe, the animals that would flourish best if left alone.

In some places there are schemes to replant trees where they have been felled for logging. In reality, however, no more than one tree is planted for every ten felled. And those replacements in no way represent the diversity of species that existed before. Instead, nowadays there are incongruous plantations of eucalyptus or pine trees where once there was a huge variety of important species living side by side. It is such variety that is vital to sustain animals such as gibbons.

SLASH AND BURN

Another principal reason for forest clearance is agriculture. Often after the forests have been superficially cleared by the logging practices, local people go in and indulge in a system known as slash and burn. This involves cutting down the remaining trees and shrubs, then clearing the undergrowth by burning. The resulting ashes provide the land with instant nutrients and an illusory fertility.

For a few years, peasant farmers cultivate the land and support their families by growing crops. However, before long the soil has been robbed of

---

EVERY YEAR VAST AREAS OF TROPICAL FORESTS THROUGHOUT SOUTHEAST ASIA ARE LOST TO LOGGING AND AGRICULTURE

---

its nutrient value, and wild plants—less demanding of rich soil—begin to invade the cultivation. Heavy rain may remove the topsoil and further leach out all goodness. Unable to turn this process around, the peasant farmers simply move on to another area to clear more forest and start again. The area left behind reverts to a sort of acid grassland, occasionally used by cattle ranchers for their stock for a few years, until it will no longer support even this level of use. In some cases, the area becomes an arid wasteland and the forest is irretrievably lost.

The Indo-Malayan subregion of Southeast Asia accounts for a significant amount of the world's tropical forests, some 832 million acres (336.5 million hectares). Vast amounts of it have already been destroyed, some 95 percent in Bangladesh, 79 percent in Thailand, and 60 percent on the island of Borneo. Approximately 2,700 square miles (7,000 square kilometers) of forest are destroyed in Indonesia each year, while nearly half of Malaya's

ENDANGERED SPECIES

THE DISAPPEARING RAIN FORESTS

The destruction of vast areas of rain forest across so much of Southeast Asia has brought about a serious decline in the numbers of all gibbon species.

At one stage, gibbons extended farther north than they do today—as far as the Yellow River in eastern China. Now the concolor gibbon is found only on the extreme southern border of China and on the Chinese island of Hainan. Here, there is a subspecies of the concolor gibbon that is found only in two wildlife sanctuaries and that, it is thought, may be on the verge of extinction. At the end of the 1980s only 30–40 individuals were thought to be alive—scarcely enough to form a viable breeding population.

The siamang is among the most seriously affected by habitat destruction. In the mid-1970s there were thought to be somewhere short of 200,000 siamangs left, but predictions based on the rate of forest clearance thought there would only be isolated populations left by the beginning of the 1990s. The same story applies to the lar gibbon. Existing in healthy

CONSERVATION MEASURES

● Gibbons are legally protected across most, if not all, of their range. As a result, demand for animals and their parts has been greatly reduced. Illegal hunting and trade, however, still must be addressed.

One of the biggest protection programs for gibbons was set up in 1977 in South Carolina by the International Primate Protection League.

numbers—nearly three million—in the mid-1970s, there were thought to be no more than 400,000 by 1980 and, again, populations were threatened with becoming more and more isolated as time, and forest destruction, continued.

The pileated gibbon of Thailand and Cambodia is one that has suffered through being hunted for food, as well as the disruption to its habitat. There were thought to be no more than about 22,000 at the beginning of the 1980s. The plight of the kloss gibbon is more acute; its numbers were down to 3,000 by the 1980s.

Inset picture E. A. Janes/NHPA

SOME SUBSPECIES OF THE CONCOLOR GIBBON (*ABOVE*) ARE NOW ON THE VERGE OF EXTINCTION.

● In 1983 the International Tropical Timber Organization (ITTO) was formed with the aim of reducing the rate of deforestation and managing the forests on a sustainable basis. Although this is a step in the right direction, progress has been slow.

● Twycross Zoo in Leicestershire, England, helps other zoos establish captive breeding programs for pileated gibbons.

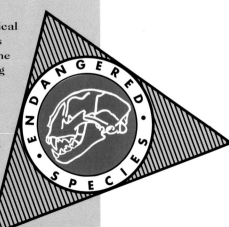

GIBBONS IN DANGER

ALL SPECIES ARE DECLINING TO A GREATER OR LESSER DEGREE AND ARE GIVEN PROTECTION ACROSS MOST OF THEIR RANGE. THE IUCN LISTS THE FOLLOWING SPECIES:

CONCOLOR GIBBON	ENDANGERED
HOOLOCK GIBBON	ENDANGERED
KLOSS GIBBON	ENDANGERED
MOLOCH GIBBON	ENDANGERED
PILEATED GIBBON	ENDANGERED

ENDANGERED MEANS THAT THE ANIMAL IS IN DANGER OF EXTINCTION AND ITS SURVIVAL IS UNLIKELY UNLESS STEPS ARE TAKEN TO SAVE IT.

rain forests have fallen to logging in the last three decades. But, tragically, it is not just commerce that has taken its toll: Over the same time span, vast tracts of rain forest in Southeast Asia have been devasted by war.

THE DEVASTATION OF WAR

The war in Cambodia and Vietnam raged over a number of years, drastically changing this area and its indigenous life—both human and animal—forever. The most vicious, far-reaching fighting of all took place during the 1970s.

Yet even before this decade there had been continuous upheaval in this area of Southeast Asia. The backlash of the conflict between North and South Vietnam was felt in Laos, Cambodia, and Thailand, and communist insurgency was rampant in Myanmar and parts of Malaysia, particularly along the border with Thailand and beyond the South China Sea. The result has been that historical boundaries have constantly shifted or vanished and former colonies have emerged as independent nations. So many were the changes during the 1960s in this region that the National Geographical Society published seven maps during that time to show redefined boundaries.

As ever during war, food was constantly in short supply. In consequence, large parts of the jungle were cleared to make paddies in an attempt to supply local people at least with the basic food staples. Whole villages were forced out of their homes and disappeared into the tangled sanctuary of the jungle to take refuge. These people, too, would have attempted to eke out an existence by clearing and cultivating land. When the criterion is to survive at all costs, human resources have little left over to consider the needs of the indigenous wildlife. Who can estimate what toll the upheavals in this part of the world had on the primates and other animal life in the jungles that comprise so much of the area?

LUCKIER THAN SOME

To some extent, gibbons have survived in areas of deforestation in Southeast Asia better than many species, despite the fact that as fruit-eaters they require a fairly extensive range in order to maintain a steady supply of ripe fruit. Their extreme specialization of locomotion—brachiation—enables them to cross quite large gaps appearing in the forest, such as newly cut roads, for example. Siamangs have fared as badly as any; their territories are smaller, so the disruption becomes greater.

Gibbons also have not fared badly at the hands of hunters as the larger ape species. To shoot such a small animal does not carry the kudos that taking a larger one has—even though, in fact, they are

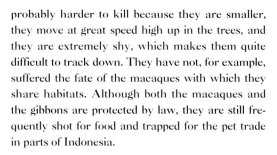

ALONGSIDE MAN

INTELLIGENCE TESTING

Gibbons have not had the same fascination for humans as the great apes, in which, through their tool-using skills and ability to learn, they perhaps see themselves more closely mirrored. Intelligence tests undertaken with gibbons have indicated that they are not as bright as other apes. But some scientists claim that these experiments did not set a fair test, as the set tasks were outside the gibbon's range of skills, involving, as they did, the need to grasp and pick up strings on the ground. This sort of skill is well within the capability of the great apes, but, because of the adaptation of gibbons' hands into "hooks" to help them swing from tree to tree, gibbons do not possess this kind of precision grip. When the tests were rerun with the strings raised so that the gibbons could more easily grasp them, they did what was required of them with ease.

The endangered moloch or silvery gibbon is found only in western Java.

probably harder to kill because they are smaller, they move at great speed high up in the trees, and they are extremely shy, which makes them quite difficult to track down. They have not, for example, suffered the fate of the macaques with which they share habitats. Although both the macaques and the gibbons are protected by law, they are still frequently shot for food and trapped for the pet trade in parts of Indonesia.

LIVING LEGENDS

Over the generations, local forest people have undoubtedly taken a few as food, although probably considerably less than other primate species, for gibbons are said to have always been somewhat revered by the forest tribes. Their similarity to man with their upright posture, family lifestyle, and facial expressions meant they were often considered to be good spirits that would bring good luck and should therefore be left to live in peace.

Certainly legends surround gibbons. One from Thailand tells of a fickle wife who helped her handsome lover kill her husband. This so angered the god Indra—the Hindu god of rain and thunder—that he turned her into a gibbon. The crimson sunrise that colors the forest sky is apparently a permanent reminder to the gibbon of this dreadful deed and one that prompts the animal to give its early morning cry, or song.

Young gibbons are said to make friendly and affectionate pets, entertaining their owners with their acrobatic antics. However, like many wild animals, as they get older, they often get increasingly unpredictable and have been known to attack their human friends. The long canine teeth can inflict considerable injury. ∎

INTO THE FUTURE

Much has been done in a number of countries around the world to help gibbons in peril. In Thailand, where it is known that gibbons are sold in the markets of Bangkok, two sanctuaries have been set up to rescue these luckless animals, some of which end up spending their lives cruelly forced to perform in backstreet bars. The sanctuary endeavors to reestablish rescued animals with a mate in a place of safety.

Until very recently, however, many captured gibbons, poached from the wild, would have slipped by, for it is known that many have been shipped illegally through Singapore to collectors around the world.

Gibbons survive well in captivity, and zoos worldwide cooperate with one another in providing mates for gibbons in order to insure their survival, at least in captivity. Twycross Zoo, in Leicestershire,

PREDICTION

UNCERTAIN FUTURE

It has been estimated that the forest resources of Malaya will be exhausted by the year 2000. And it is also thought that most species of gibbons will only exist in isolated populations in their wild habitats.

England, for example, cooperates with a number of zoos, recently with Zurich, providing them with pileated gibbons to mate with those they already possess. This is mutual cooperation with the best interests of the species in mind; the gibbons are freely given, not sold.

Twycross Zoo has around 35 gibbons, one of which they have had for longer than 30 years. They specialize in the keeping and reproduction of pileated gibbons, and recently supplied one to Blackpool Zoo to provide a mate. The gibbons are kept in their family groups in the zoos until the young ones become sexually mature.

In this way there are a number of captive-breeding programs in existence for gibbons, but unlike similar plans involving other species, it is not realistic to attempt to return them to the wild. The gibbons' almost unique lifestyle of existing in small family groups makes release projects difficult, but, more cogently, there simply is not enough wild habitat left to support any more gibbons. ■

The International Primate Protection League Sanctuary opened in South Carolina in 1977 to offer protection and care to gibbons that were being badly treated or discarded in the United States. At the time, gibbons were being used extensively in medical research, in particular for research into cancer. The University of California was granted a license entitling scientists to kill 10 gibbons a year in the course of their research there, and the sanctuary petitioned hard to have this revoked. In fact, they failed in this attempt, but the publicity about the plight of the gibbons, coupled with the general awareness of conservation, caused the research unit to be closed down. A number of the gibbons ended up at the sanctuary.

Today the sanctuary houses some 25 or so gibbons. Besides those that have come to them after being used for medical research, there are those that had been kept as pets—a practice that is now illegal in the United States—and discarded, and some that had been held in private collections, then put up for sale when the owners died. Many of these gibbons were in an extremely bad way when they arrived, displaying deeply disturbed and highly upsetting behavior. However, in the care of the sanctuary, they soon revived and flourished. The sanctuary prides itself on being an "open door," ready to take in any gibbons in peril.

The gibbons are kept in pairs or small family groups in large enclosures, some 50 ft (15 m) long, that have swing ropes and an indoor housing unit. Many have lived happily at the sanctuary for some time and have bred successfully.

Illustration Evi Antoniou

GIRAFFES

RELATIONS

Giraffes and okapis belong to the large and diverse order Artiodactyla. Other members of the order include:

PIGS & PECCARIES

HIPPOPOTAMUSES

CAMELS

DEER

WILD CATTLE

ANTELOPES

CHEVROTAINS

L. Migdale/ZEFA

The giraffe and okapi belong to the order of hoofed mammals called Artiodactyla. Together with the pronghorn and various members of the Bovidae family, such as chevrotains and deer, they are considered to be the most advanced animals in this order and are placed in the suborder Ruminantia.

ORDER

Artiodactyla
(artiodactyls)

SUBORDER

Ruminantia
(ruminants)

FAMILY

Giraffidae
(giraffes)

GIRAFFE GENUS

Giraffa

SPECIES

camelopardalis

OKAPI GENUS

Okapia

SPECIES

johnstoni

BROWSING GIANTS

THE ONLY TWO REMAINING MEMBERS OF THE SAME FAMILY, THE GIRAFFE AND OKAPI SHARE FEW COMMON FEATURES. THEY LIVE IN DIFFERENT HABITATS AND HAVE DIFFERENT LIFESTYLES

Quietly content in the company of impalas, zebras, gnu, rhinoceroses, and ostriches, the giraffe is a peaceful yet distinctive inhabitant of Africa's parklands or thornbush country. It is head and neck above all its fellow grassland dwellers, for this is the world's tallest living animal—even a newborn calf stands nearly 6 ft (1.8 m) high.

The giraffe's nearest relative, the elusive okapi, is a less familiar figure, living alone as it does in the densest parts of central Africa's equatorial forest.

The giraffe's shape is unmistakable. Its body, seemingly far too small for its long legs, slopes sharply upward from the tail base toward the incredibly long neck, which has a short, erect mane of dark hairs along its length. The relatively small head is crowned by a pair of short, sometimes tufted horns, often with a smaller one between them. The distinctive coat is an intricate network of pale-colored hair enclosing darker, irregularly shaped

Looking like crossed swords, young bulls embark on a "necking" session to determine who is boss.

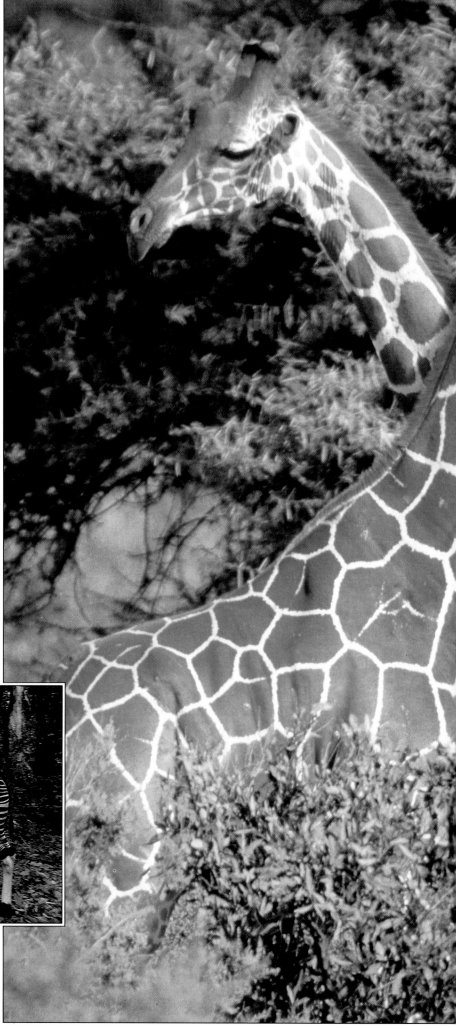

patches, and although giraffes in one area may display similar coat patterns and markings, there are always subtle differences that remain throughout the animal's life and act as a personal identification system.

The okapi is an altogether better proportioned animal, looking almost more like a zebra than its closest relative. While its legs and neck are both quite long, they are nowhere near as long as those of the giraffe—in fact they are no longer than those of many antelope—and while its body, too, slopes

---

THE COAT PATTERNS OF GIRAFFES ARE AS INDIVIDUAL AS FINGERPRINTS—NO TWO ARE EVER THE SAME

---

down toward the hindquarters, the angle is not so acute. The okapi's body is also larger and more thickset in proportion to the legs. The coat is a rich purplish red, sometimes almost black, but it, too, has a distinctive pattern: striking white stripes of varied widths that traverse the flanks and upper legs. The male has a pair of horns.

Features shared by both giraffe and okapi are short, sleek hair; large, dark eyes; relatively large, rounded, mobile ears; a tail reaching to the hocks and ending in a long tuft of hairs; and an incredibly long, extensible tongue. That of the giraffe may measure nearly 20 in (50 cm), while the okapi can curl the tongue upward to wash around its eyes.

The giraffe and okapi are even-toed ungulates—that is, each foot has become modified during the course of evolution to end in two evenly sized

The okapi (above) *is a shy and elusive denizen of forest habitats such as this one in Zaire.*

Jeanne Drake/Tony Stone Worldwide

● **The okapi is one of the world's most recently discovered mammals. It was first described in 1901 when naturalist Sir Harry Johnston found specimens in the Congo. It was accordingly given its scientific name *Okapia johnstoni*.**

● **The giraffe's blood pressure is two to three times greater than human's—probably the highest of any living animal.**

● **The giraffe has the largest brain of all hoofed animals.**

hoofed digits. Both animals are ruminants—herbivores that regurgitate partly digested food to be chewed again, known as chewing the cud.

LIVING THE HIGH LIFE

Although the giraffe's great height gives it access to food no other animal can reach, this stature also presents physical problems. Blood must be pumped a considerable distance—all the way up the neck—to reach the brain; to achieve this the heart is exceptionally large and thick-muscled. However, if the blood was then to be pumped into the brain at

THE GIRAFFE HAS SUPERB SIGHT, SAID TO BE ACUTE OVER A DISTANCE OF 0.6 MILES (1 KM). IT CAN ALSO SEE COLORS

the same pressure, the brain would be damaged. To reduce that pressure, the blood is spread through a large network of vessels before entering the brain. Also, when the giraffe lowers its head, as it does when it drinks, it would run into problems if the blood were to rush into the skull. To prevent this, there is a series of valves throughout the giraffe's veins and arteries that controls the flow of blood. The animal's lungs are remarkably large, to compensate for the increased volume of air in the long windpipe.

OUTSIZED ANCESTORS

As a group, even-toed ungulates first evolved and radiated in the Eocene period, which dates from 54 million years ago, but it was not until the Miocene era—beginning some 26 million years ago—that the direct ancestors of the giraffes appeared. They made their appearance in Europe and Africa and, as time went on, two distinct lineages evolved. One was characterized by long-necked, high-browsing animals, while the other featured shorter-necked, or low-level, animals that nevertheless were still browsers rather than grazers.

As the first great grass plains emerged in Africa, during the Pliocene era—between seven and two million years ago—so evolved numbers of giraffids. One was *Paleotragus* (pal-ee-o-TRAH-gus), which had two small horns above its eyes and stripes over its back, legs, and flanks. Today's okapi looks remarkably similar to *Paleotragus*, although some species of this prehistoric ancestor stood nearly twice as tall.

A more recent ancestor (see box below) was *Sivatherium* (siv-a-THARE-ee-um), which shared its environment with another extinct species, *Giraffokeryx* (gyr-aff-o-KARE-iks), which had two pairs of small horns—one pair above the eyes and the other situated in a line down the center of the face. This was another animal to have striped markings similar to today's okapi. Its neck was noticeably longer than that of *Sivatherium*. ■

ANCESTORS

One of the most recent ancestors of the giraffe and okapi, *Sivatherium* roamed Europe, Africa, and southern Asia less than two million years ago. In fact, many of the earlier giraffids looked more similar to today's species than did *Sivatherium*. With its short, thick neck and legs, and long, branched horns, it was more reminiscent of a moose. However, it also possessed two much smaller horns just above the eyes, similar to those of the giraffe and okapi.

GIRAFFE
Giraffa camelopardalis
(Gi-RAF-a cam-el-o-par-dah-lis)

Scientists agree that there are various subspecies of giraffes, although they argue about the exact number. Commonly, there are considered to be eight subspecies (see below). Some scientists claim there are only three subspecies, while others think there may be as many as twelve. Grouped according to location, the subspecies are distinguished only by their different coat patterns; all other features and characteristics are identical. However, it should also be noted that widely differing patterns can be found in giraffes belonging to the same subspecies.

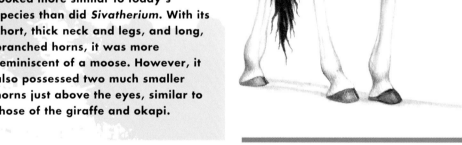

SUGGESTED SUBSPECIES:
RETICULATED GIRAFFE
ROTHSCHILD'S GIRAFFE
MASAI GIRAFFE
SOUTHERN GIRAFFE
THORNICROFT'S GIRAFFE
NUBIAN GIRAFFE
KORDOFAN GIRAFFE
ANGOLAN GIRAFFE

PIGS

HIPPOS

PECCARIES

BOVIDS

ARTIODACTYLA
(EVEN-TOED UNGULATES)

Illustrations Ruth Grewcock

THE GIRAFFE'S FAMILY TREE

The giraffe and okapi belong to one of the largest orders of mammals. About one-third of all known mammals are herbivores, and more than half of these belong to the orders Perissodactyla and Artiodactyla—odd- and even-toed ungulates respectively. The Perissodactyla order contains only six genera, while the Artiodactyla has around eighty genera. The giraffe and okapi are most closely related to the families Tragulidae, Antilocapridae, Cervidae, and Bovidae. The Bovidae has the most number of specie, and is considered to be the dominant group of artiodactyls.

OKAPI
Okapia johnstoni
(ok-AH-pee-a john-STONE-ey)

Much less well known than the giraffe, the single species of okapi has been known to science only from the beginning of the 20th century. It is extremely wary and elusive, dashing into the thickest forest at the first sign of intruders, making studies of it in the wild very difficult. Unusual among mammals, the male is smaller than the female.

Color illustrations Evi Antoniou

DEER

CAMELS

LLAMAS

CHEVROTAINS

X
R A Y

The long neck of the giraffe has only seven vertebrae, the same as other mammals. However, each one is greatly elongated and articulated with ball-and-socket joints, allowing great flexibility. The size, together with the dorsal spines on the fourth and fifth vertebrae, give an anchorage for the large muscles that support the head and neck.

neck

GIRAFFE SKELETON

two digits on each foot

A feature of the giraffe's skull, particularly the males, is the continuous accumulation of bone over the facial area, manifesting itself as knobs at the base of the skull, over the eyes, centrally on the forehead, and sometimes on the back of the skull. An older adult male has a massive clublike head that, as a potentially effective weapon, helps give dominance over younger animals.

GIRAFFE SKULL

splayed canine teeth

GIRAFFE HOOVES

rear hoof

front hoof

Central wrist or anklebones are absent; the third and fourth digits have developed and finish in two large, even-sized hooves. The remaining digits have virtually disappeared during the course of evolution.

ANATOMY:
THE GIRAFFE

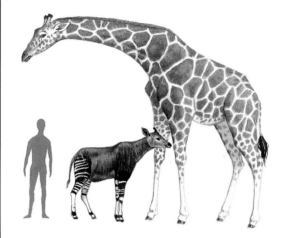

An adult male giraffe may stand up to 18 ft (5.4 m) high—almost twice the height of an elephant—and if he stretches his limbs and neck he can add another 18 in (45 cm) to this. The thicker-set okapi (above center) is considerably smaller at a maximum height of 7 ft (2.15 m).

THE TORSO

The torso is relatively small compared to the length of the legs and neck, with the shoulder much higher than the croup, so that the back slopes down to the tail. The additional height to the front of the body is mainly due to the heavy muscular development around the neck. The deep chest houses the enlarged lungs.

LEGS AND FEET

The giraffe's legs are extremely long, but in spite of the fact that the body slopes down toward the tail, the front legs are only fractionally longer than the hind. At a walk, in particular, there appears to be little flexion in each step, resulting in a somewhat stiff-legged gait. The feet are very large. In the giraffe the hooves are 6 in (15 cm) high in males and 4 in (10 cm) high in females. The okapi has scent-secreting glands in the hooves; these are absent in the giraffe.

BONY APPENDAGES

No other animal has horns like those of the giraffe and okapi. A calf is born with a pair of cartilaginous knobs, which initially are unattached to the skull. Later they begin to ossify (turn into bone), fusing with the skull. Although they grow slowly, they rarely exceed 5.3 in (13.5 cm). Throughout the life of the animal, the horns are covered with skin and hair, although the latter sometimes wears away from the apex. The okapi has one pair of horns, present in the male only.

CLASSIFICATION

GENUS: *GIRAFFA*

SPECIES: *CAMELOPARDALIS*

SIZE

HEAD-BODY LENGTH/MALE: 12–15 FT (3.8–4.7 M)

HEIGHT/MALE: 15–18 FT (4.7–5.5 M)

WEIGHT/MALE: 1,764–4,255 LB (800–1,930 KG)

HEIGHT AT BIRTH/MALE: 6 FT 3 IN (1.9 M)

WEIGHT AT BIRTH/MALE: 225 LB (102 KG)

ADULT MALES ARE LARGER THAN FEMALES

COLORATION

BACKGROUND COLOR VARIES FROM PALE ORANGE TO ALMOST BLACK

COAT PATTERNS VARY FROM LARGE, REGULAR CHESTNUT SHAPES TO JAGGED PATCHES

BACKGROUND COLOR BROKEN BY NARROW, PURE WHITE LINES INTO IRREGULAR PATTERNS

FEATURES

LONG BLACK TONGUE THAT CAN BE EXTENDED TO 18 IN (46 CM)

BONY APPENDAGES ON HEAD THAT ARE MORE PRONOUNCED IN MALES

LARGE BROWN EYES

LONG TAIL OF ABOUT 30–40 IN (76–101 CM) WITH TASSEL ON TIP

SPLAYED CANINE TEETH TO HELP ANIMAL "COMB" FOLIAGE

EYES

The large brown eyes are set wide on the head to give a remarkable field of vision. Eyesight is also the most highly developed of the senses in the giraffe. The eyes are protected by long, full lashes.

TONGUE

The black tongue of both the giraffe and okapi is extensible and very long. It is adapted for plucking leaves as these animals browse selectively. Both animals also use the tongue for grooming.

NUBIAN COAT PATTERN

KENYAN COAT PATTERN

Color and pattern vary according to the subspecies and also to each individual, but they essentially comprise a latticework of pale hairs enclosing usually irregular-shaped blotches of a darker color. This may vary from golden to rich liver-red and tends to darken with age.

HOW A GIRAFFE MOVES

A giraffe appears stiff-legged when moving. Its pace can be described as a "rack," in that the front and back legs on each side of the body are moved almost in unison, the forefoot leaving the ground just in front of the hind one. This is an unusual gait, but one that works. A giraffe in full flight can run at 37 mph (60 km/h).

SYMBOLS OF THE SAVANNA

To MOST PEOPLE, THE STATELY GIRAFFE IS THE ANIMAL THAT IS MOST CHARACTERISTIC OF THE AFRICAN GRASSLANDS; ITS CLOSEST RELATIVE, THE SHY, FOREST-DWELLING OKAPI, IS RARELY SEEN

The two living species of the giraffid family are both found only in Africa, where they are essentially woodland browsers. However, while the giraffe inhabits shrubby savanna, the okapi is found only in heavy forest, which is shunned by the giraffe. By and large, the giraffe is a social mammal, living in loosely associated groups; the okapi, on the other hand, leads a solitary existence.

Both the giraffe and okapi are principally diurnal animals, although the giraffe is known to sleep for no more than four hours in a 24-hour period. Its greatest periods of activity are for about three hours shortly after dawn and a similar amount of time just before dusk, when it feeds avidly.

During the hot midday period, the giraffe tends to rest, lazily chewing the cud. This is often done standing up—indeed, it quite often even sleeps

IN STUDIES OF SERENGETI GIRAFFES, THE SAME COMPOSITION OF A GROUP OCCURED ONLY TWICE OVER 24 HOURS

standing up. Occasionally, the giraffe rests sitting down—legs folded beneath its body—but it seldom lets its neck rest on the ground, preferring instead to hold it erect. During the night, the giraffe sleeps lying down for short periods—usually for no more than five minutes or so. Then the animal curls up and rests its head on the lower part of a hind leg or on the rump. A good proportion of the hours of darkness, however, are spent chewing the cud; if it is a particularly bright, moonlit night, the giraffe will also browse.

That the giraffe is so entirely suited to its environment is shown by the fact that, even when it is resting in the heat of the midday sun, it rarely seeks out the shade. Instead, it is entirely happy to stand

in the open, often the only animal to be seen so exposed. It is the giraffe's large body surface that allows such heat tolerance. The giraffe does not scratch in dust, neither does it wallow in mud the way a rhinoceros, hippopotamus, or elephant does. Indeed, being a poor wader and unable to swim, it shuns water except for drinking. The okapi, on the other hand, readily cools off by taking a "shower" in a water hole, licking itself dry again with its long tongue.

Almost the only concession the giraffe makes to grooming seems to be to rub its body on trees, and this is probably to rid itself of troublesome ticks. It also licks itself with its long black tongue. Generally, it is a quiet animal, and even though it is known to have a repertoire of sounds, it rarely utters them. Moaning, rumbling, grunting, hissing, and coughing noises have all been reported, and it is known to give a snorting alarm call when danger threatens. Most of the time, however, the only noise to be heard in the presence of a group of giraffes is the gentle clicking of their hooves as

Nicholas Parfitt/Tony Stone Worldwide

A reticulated giraffe (below) *resting during the heat of the day in Tsavo, Kenya. The young are most vulnerable to predators during such rest periods.*

Dieter & Mary Plage/Survival Anglia

A small group of giraffes (above) *in the shade of trees in Ruaha National Park, Tanzania.*

An okapi (left) *taking a bath. At the other end, the tail is swished to deter biting insects.*

they lift their feet clear of the ground. Equally, the okapi appears to have a range of vocalizations, but these do not seem an important part of communication, except between cows and calves. It does tend to snort when angry or when under attack.

In spite of its enormous height, and its predilection for open country, a giraffe is often remarkably difficult to spot in the grasslands. Visitors on safari often find that what at first seemed to be a few trees near the track make unexpectedly giraffelike movements. One of the surprising things about such a group is the diversity of sizes in the animals; an adult bull can stand 3.2 ft (1 m) or more taller than the cows and will tower over any calves. Giraffes themselves are always on the alert, their superb vision warning them of intruders when they are still some distance away. If need be, they will flee, shepherding any young calves ahead of the adults. Calves are capable of keeping up with their elders from a very early age. ∎

HABITATS

The giraffe and okapi occupy different areas of the African landscape, never crossing one another's path. The giraffe keeps mainly to the grasslands, although it ranges from those that are sparsely wooded to areas of more thickly overgrown scrubland or bush country. Very occasionally, giraffes are found at the edge of a forest, but they will venture into fairly dense vegetation only where it borders a river. Ill at ease in water, the giraffe stays clear of rivers—however shallow—so a stretch of water often marks the border of a home range.

There are two keys to a giraffe's environment: the presence of thorn acacia trees and firm ground. Acacia forms the giraffe's staple diet, and the trees grow up to elevations of about 6,600 ft (2,000 m). Firm ground is essential because—unlike its distant relative the camel, an even-toed ungulate that is well adapted to walking on soft, shifting sands—the giraffe's long legs have to support a relatively heavy body and the animal quickly becomes bogged down on soft or swampy terrain. Its enormous feet sink rapidly into soft ground, making movement difficult.

The giraffe is reasonably common south of the Sahara to eastern Transvaal, Natal, and northern Botswana, and it has been reintroduced to game reserves in South Africa.

Clem Haagner/Ardea

 **SIGHT**

MUTUAL BENEFITS

The massive giraffe has one tiny but pernicious enemy—the troublesome tick that plagues it throughout its life. Its way of dealing with this is to stand over a 6-ft- (2-m-) high bush and rock itself backward and forward in an attempt to dislodge the ticks from its belly region, where the hair is at its thinnest. However, nature has provided another solution; oxpecker birds, also known as tick birds, are often seen perched on the backs and necks of giraffes, pecking at the ticks and other skin parasites— thereby gaining a tasty meal while fulfilling a much needed service to the giraffe. Such mutually beneficial relationships in the animal world are known as symbiotic partnerships. Besides ridding the host of the ticks, an oxpecker will also give an alarm call if a predator approaches.

K. & K. Ammann/Planet Earth Pictures

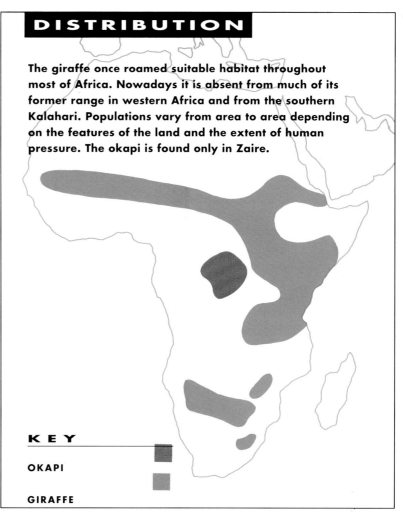

DISTRIBUTION

The giraffe once roamed suitable habitat throughout most of Africa. Nowadays it is absent from much of its former range in western Africa and from the southern Kalahari. Populations vary from area to area depending on the features of the land and the extent of human pressure. The okapi is found only in Zaire.

KEY

OKAPI

GIRAFFE

Animals converging on a drinking hole in the Etosha National Park, Namibia (above). The giraffe splays its legs awkwardly in order to reach the precious commodity. The elephant and ostriches will have no such problem.

A yellow-billed oxpecker helps itself to a meal of ticks (left), at the same time ridding the giraffe of an aggravating parasite.

KEY FACTS

● **At the end of the 1970s it was estimated that there were about 6,000 giraffes in some 5,000 sq mi (12,950 sq km) of the Serengeti.**

● **Some anthropologists believe that it was in the giraffe's homeland—the African savanna—that early man first adopted an upright stance. This enabled him to hunt more efficiently and to keep a lookout for predators above the tall grassland.**

● **The Serengeti is home to more than 100 species of mammals and some 200 species of birds.**

● **The acacia, one of the giraffe's favorite foodstuffs, is the most typical tree of the African grassland.**

The okapi, on the other hand, lives only in Zaire, in the mixed forest belt of the northern, eastern, and southern Congo basin, bounded in the west by flood forest. Within the Ubangi, Uele, Aruwimi, and Ituri rain forests, it is found only at lowland depths, generally near streams and rivers. It tends to avoid very swampy areas, but it will splash across shallow water if need be. Within the dense, damp forests, it moves along regularly used, well-trodden paths, fleeing into the dense jungle at the least disturbance. With hearing the best developed of its senses, it quickly detects any danger.

HARMONIOUS GRAZERS

Not only does the giraffe share its environment with one of the richest diversities of animal wildlife to be found anywhere, but many of its fellow grassland dwellers are also hoofed animals—herbivores that could, therefore, compete with one another for available food. In fact, harmony reigns, for evolution has seen to it that the various species have different food preferences. The giraffe is exclusively a browser, plucking leaves from trees that are way out of reach of most other browsing animals.

Antelope and black rhinoceroses browse lower branches, while wildebeests and zebras—grazing animals—crop the grasses. Even at ground level, grazers feed on different types of grass, keeping competition to a minimum.

FORMIDABLE IN DEFENSE

The giraffe's great size, its superior eyesight (it has the greatest range of vision of any land animal), its surprising turn of speed, and the fact that its hooves are lethal weapons render it largely invulnerable to predators. The only time a healthy adult giraffe is at risk is when it splays its long forelegs by a watering hole to drink; then it is not unknown for a lion or even a crocodile to seize the opportunity to grab hold of the giraffe's head and strangle or suffocate it. While browsing, a group of giraffes is constantly alert, and if they spot a lion, they keep it in their field of vision, even moving around to insure it does not creep up on them unawares. A lion hesitates to attack prey that is aware it is being stalked.

If directly threatened, a giraffe kicks out with its legs to deliver a crushing blow capable, reportedly, of decapitating a lion. All its limbs make excellent defensive weapons, the hind feet delivering a conventional kick and the forelegs being used either to

give a forward chop-kick or a strike with the whole stiff leg. Calves are much more vulnerable than the adults and a considerable number are taken by lions, wild dogs, and hyenas. Young okapis fall victim to the golden cat, and also possibly to the shy serval, with which they share their forest environment. Only leopards are a threat to adult okapis.

Unlike many of the ungulates with which it shares its grasslands, the giraffe is not a migrant. Concentrations have been observed near rivers in the dry season, and their movement rarely exceeds a distance of 12–18 miles (20–30 kilometers). ■

FOCUS ON
THE SERENGETI

The Serengeti National Park is the largest and probably the best known of Tanzania's national parks. It is characterized by vast open plains, acacia and savanna woodland, and scrub areas, with tree-lined rivers and high rocky outcrops, and there is some swampy ground. There are two alkaline lakes in the south, which sometime dry up. In the wet season, their full waters attract a mass of waterbirds, including flamingos.

The Serengeti is home to the greatest concentration of game animals found anywhere in the world, including wildebeests, hartebeests, duikers, steinboks, gazelles, antelope, kudu, eland, buffalo, zebras, and rhinoceroses. There are all sorts of wildcats—the cheetah, caracal, African wildcat, serval, and leopard; above all, the Serengeti is renowned for its lion population. Visitors report seeing 40 or more lions in a day.

Many animals are migratory visitors, coming into the park when the seasonal rains have brought rich growths of short, succulent grass. The new growth is characterized by stems no more than 6 in (15 cm) long; it is particularly palatable to grazing animals. Naturally, the great droves of herbivores lured to this food also attract numbers of predators. Hyenas, for example, are common during the rains, but they tend to move on in search of other prey as the Serengeti dries out.

TEMPERATURE AND RAINFALL

| TEMPERATURE |
| RAINFALL |

AVERAGE MONTHLY TEMPERATURE °F: 86, 77, 68, 59, 50, 41, 32

AVERAGE MONTHLY RAINFALL (in): 9.6, 8.0, 6.4, 4.8, 3.2, 1.6, 0

Months: JAN, FEB, MAR, APR, MAY, JUN, JUL, AUG, SEP, OCT, NOV, DEC

Many hoofed animals migrate from the Serengeti in the dry season, with hungry predators following hard on their heels. But the giraffe never roams far and seems able to cope with the heat.

NEIGHBORS

The Serengeti is home to thousands of animals. Some of the hoofed species are annual visitors that take advantage of the lush grasses after the heavy rains.

GNU

Also called wildebeests, these grazing antelope flock to the Serengeti in thousands.

COBRA

Cobras are venomous snakes with front fangs. They are found all over Africa except in the Sahara.

Illustrations Joanne Cowne. Elisabeth Smith: oxpecker, secretary bird, lion, and spotted hyena

SERENGETI NATIONAL PARK

The Serengeti National Park lies on the Serengeti Plain at an elevation of 2,950–6,400 ft (900–1,800 m). It covers an area of 5,600 sq miles (14,500 sq km) and is bounded on the north by Kenya's Masai Mara Game Park.

SERENGETI

LION
The most abundant of the Serengeti predators, it targets baby giraffes during the breeding season.

CROCODILE
The crocodile will only attack a giraffe in its most vulnerable position—when stooping at a water hole.

SPOTTED HYENA
A young giraffe is no match for the bone-crushing power in the jaws of these pack hunters.

MODERATELY DANGEROUS

MODERATELY DANGEROUS

MODERATELY DANGEROUS

Adrian Warren/Ardea

THOMSON'S GAZELLE

Agile and graceful, this gazelle is the favorite prey of many large predators, including lions.

IMPALA

Female impala live in large herds, accompanied by only one adult male. Young males often form bachelor herds.

TERMITE

The highly social termite is one of nature's great builders; its homes are often elaborate structures.

OXPECKER

This bird is a member of the starling family. It lives on a diet of insects that are parasitic on large mammals.

SECRETARY BIRD

This bird of prey feasts on snakes. Its scaly legs protect it from their bites.

FOOD AND FEEDING

The most consistent browsing animal of the grasslands, the giraffe is a highly selective feeder, eating mainly the leaves, buds, and shoots of trees—the acacia in particular, but also mimosa and wild apricot trees.

Being a ruminant, the giraffe has a stomach with four compartments. The food is picked, chewed peremptorily, and swallowed quickly, entering the first compartment, which is the rumen. After a softening process, it is regurgitated as a bolus (lump of masticated food) into the mouth—strong muscles in the esophagus push it back up the neck—where it is chewed once more. After this it is swallowed again, and it passes through the second, third, and finally fourth compartments. The greatest digestive activity takes place in the fourth compartment, called the abomasum. This type of digestion system enables ruminants to extract all available nutrients from their fibrous diet.

DEALING WITH A THORNY MEAL
Other adaptations to the giraffe's chosen diet include bristly lips—the upper of which is particularly flexible—a long tongue, a heavily grooved roof of the mouth, extremely viscous saliva, splayed-out canines and low-crowned molars, and, of course,

IT HAS BEEN ESTIMATED THAT GIRAFFES CHEW EACH BOLUS OF CUD ABOUT **44** TIMES AT A RATE OF ONE CHEW A SECOND

the animal's height, combined with a modified atlas-axis joint in the neck that allows the head to tilt to the vertical. The acacia is a very thorny tree, but the giraffe's bristly lips seem impervious to the thorns' sharpness. Mixed into the thick saliva, the thistles are soon compressed against the ridged palate, allowing the giraffe to swallow them painlessly. The extensible tongue, which, like the lips, is bristled, gathers the leaves, and the giraffe usually plucks them by holding them firmly in its mouth and then pulling its head away from the branch. The low-crowned molars make ideal grinding surfaces, while the splayed canines prove useful for browsing thornless shrubs: The shoots are pulled through the mouth and the leaves stripped off neatly by lobes on the canines.

KEY FACTS

● **Although acacia is undoubtedly the favorite food of giraffes, more than 100 plants have been recorded as being included in their diet. The sweet pulp of young shoots attracts a type of stinging ant, but the giraffe is impervious to it. The ant plays an important part in the dispersal of seeds.**

● **During a 24-hour period a cow usually spends about 55 percent of her time in active grazing; a bull spends 43 percent. Although a bull consumes a larger bulk, the cow actually has a greater relative intake of food per body weight, helping to insure that she remains in prime breeding condition.**

● **The giraffe's low-crowned molars are unique among mammals. They are wrinkled and ridged, providing a rough surface; in most other mammals the enamel is smooth.**

AT WATER
Giraffes look awkward and ungainly while drinking; because of the high water content in their food, they do not need to visit water as often as other animals.

All illustrations Simon Turvey/Wildlife Art Agency.

The giraffe's great height gives it access to high foliage way out of the reach of other animals, and bulls, which are often 3 ft (90 cm) or more taller than cows, can reach even higher into a tree. Watching a group of giraffes browsing from a distance, it is possible to tell the sexes apart by their feeding methods. A male typically stands with head and neck stretched fully up to the shoots, perhaps on the underside of a high canopy. A female, on the other hand, more usually curls her neck over to feed at body- or even knee-height, plucking leaves from the crown of much lower trees or shrubs. More readily than a female, the males will often enter denser wooded areas where the trees grow taller than out in the open grassland. This means that even between the different sexes of giraffes there is less competition for exactly the same foodstuffs.

The giraffe selects foliage that has a considerably higher nutritive value than that consumed by many herbivores, but it also occasionally eats plants, flowers, seed pods, and fruits. It also sometimes eats the soil, particularly where the savanna floor is salty or full of minerals the animal otherwise lacks in its diet. Cows feed for

LIQUID INTAKE

Giraffes get much of the water they need from the foliage they eat. Acacia twigs, for instance, are made up of more than 70 percent water. In the dry season giraffes browse around trees near water that continue to produce new foliage.

longer than bulls each day, but they are actually more selective, always picking the most nutritious foliage. Bulls eat a greater bulk but spend more time ruminating and walking around, usually in search of a female ready to breed. The female's greater nutritional intake per body weight keeps her as healthy as she can be for breeding and giving her young the best possible start in life.

Also a ruminant, the okapi, too, is a selective feeder that gathers its food in much the same way—using its long, extensible tongue and particularly mobile lips. It includes leaves, buds, shoots, ferns, fruit, and fungi in its diet and is particularly fond of euphorbia plants, which are poisonous to humans. It, too, will nibble at mineral-rich earths, particularly those with a high charcoal content. ■

VULNERABILITY WHEN DRINKING

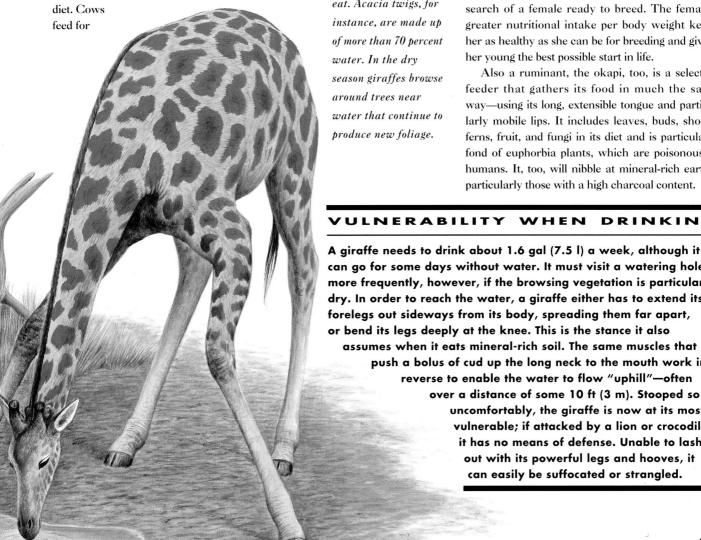

A giraffe needs to drink about 1.6 gal (7.5 l) a week, although it can go for some days without water. It must visit a watering hole more frequently, however, if the browsing vegetation is particularly dry. In order to reach the water, a giraffe either has to extend its forelegs out sideways from its body, spreading them far apart, or bend its legs deeply at the knee. This is the stance it also assumes when it eats mineral-rich soil. The same muscles that push a bolus of cud up the long neck to the mouth work in reverse to enable the water to flow "uphill"—often over a distance of some 10 ft (3 m). Stooped so uncomfortably, the giraffe is now at its most vulnerable; if attacked by a lion or crocodile, it has no means of defense. Unable to lash out with its powerful legs and hooves, it can easily be suffocated or strangled.

SOCIAL STRUCTURE

Although undoubtedly a social animal, the giraffe cannot be described as a herd animal like many ungulates. It is said that the individual is the basic social unit in giraffe society—animals come together in loose associations in which the only bonds that are in any way permanent are those between mother and calf. In the days when giraffes were much more numerous than today, groups of more than 100 animals would roam and browse together; nowadays these most frequently number six to a dozen.

Because the composition of such groups is constantly changing, there is no basic core and, by and large, each individual remains physically and socially aloof. The center of the group may be a mother and calf, or the whole group may comprise young males or young females. At any time a group of males may mingle for a day with a group of females with their young. Although there is a dominance hierarchy, there is no leader of the group and there is no apparently coordinated movement. Older bulls become increasingly solitary as the years go by and spend much of their time checking around the females in their home range to see if any are receptive to breeding.

> A MATURE BULL GIRAFFE HAS BEEN KNOWN TO KNOCK AN OPPONENT SENSELESS WITH A BLOW FROM HIS HEAD

The main purpose of these loose associations, it seems, is for protection against predators, and because of both their acuity and great range of vision, giraffes in different groups can keep in visual contact over great distances. If there is no imminent danger, such a group may actually browse over an area of half a mile (0.8 km) or more; individuals in a group will often stand chewing the cud at distances of up to 65 ft (20 m) apart.

Although nonterritorial, giraffes do have a home range. This varies in size according to location, season, and sex. Ranges have been known to be as small as 2 sq miles (5 sq km) and larger than 250 sq miles (650 sq km). Around 62 sq miles (160 sq km) seems to be a rough average in many areas, with the size varying little between male and female, although mature bulls often confine themselves to a smaller area, while younger bulls that are still seeking to establish some kind of range may wander farther afield.

Within this range there is a "central core" area in which the animals spend most of their time, and

GIRAFFE HORNS *have evolved as weapons, but they are used only in ritualized fighting. Serious blows are aimed with the heavy, clublike heads.*

NECKING GIRAFFES

When they reach three or four years old, male giraffes begin to flex their muscles in an attempt to climb up the dominance ladder. To this end, they begin challenging one another, indulging in what may be seen as a ritualized duel. As with older bulls, such an encounter begins with the young giraffes facing each other as they pull themselves up to full height. Then they approach each other, either head-on or one coming up alongside his opponent. In almost slow motion, they begin to rub their heads and necks together, intertwining necks and delivering soft blows with the head—the most strenuous movement coming from the ears, which flap to and fro continually. They may also lean against each other, rubbing shoulders and flanks, which actually allows them to assess the strength of an opponent. Although these fights do not achieve anything, the "winner" is usually the one that remains the most erect throughout, and it will often climb on the back of the loser to display its dominance.

Illustrations Andie Peck/Wildlife Art Agency

A hunting party of hungry lions patiently waits for the giraffe to leave her dead calf. They will eventually get their meal.

which provides most of their feeding requirements. When a giraffe strays into the outer area—an area known as the buffer zone in that it is still familiar and provides a "buffer" to the unknown world beyond—its behavior becomes noticeably more alert and agitated, with more vigilance required.

When observing a widely spread-out group of browsing or ruminating giraffes, it may seem that they have little to do with one another, but they do in fact interact and recognize relative statuses within a dominance hierarchy. With cows this hierarchy is very low-key and generally amounts to no more than who has the best place while browsing a tree. A cow finding herself displaced, however, will simply move on to browse nearby.

There is usually a dominant bull within the core area of a home range that has the pick of the cows; he will both challenge and be challenged by others. Fighting that can occur among bulls is an extension of the ritualized fighting, known as necking (see box, p. 824), which tends to

Jonathan Scott/Planet Earth Pictures

BULLS' HEADS
The head of an adult 15-year-old bull can weigh up to 15.5 lb (7 kg) more than a male half his age.

occur between younger bulls as they begin to try to determine dominance.

An encounter between two older bulls usually begins with an initial threat display in which they face each other, raising heads and standing as tall as they can. Often the less dominant one becomes submissive at this point. If the fighting continues, the more mature bull has the greater advantage; the older the animal, the more bone it will have on its skull, making its head a veritable club capable of delivering a staggering blow. Luckily, serious confrontations tend to be infrequent.

THE SOLITARY OKAPI
Very little is known about the okapi's life in the wild. It seems that these animals are considerably more solitary than the giraffe, adult males and females coming together only at breeding time. That they have a network of well-used paths within their forest home, coupled with the fact that they have scent glands on their feet and have been reported spraying bushes with urine, indicates a more territorial nature than that of the giraffe. ∎

REPRODUCTION

Very few studies of reproduction in the okapi have been conducted in the wild. It seems, however, that they can produce young at any time of the year but do so mainly between May and June and between November and December. The interval between calving is usually 15 to 17 months.

From studies in captivity it is known that females remain receptive for a month or so at a time and advertise this by calling as well as scent marking with urine. Courtship behavior appears to be similar to that of certain antelope; females circle around a male who, besides exhibiting the *flehmen* reaction (see Life Cycle, p. 828), indulges in behavior known as the *Laufschlag*, in which he touches the female's underbelly with a stiff foreleg, both before and after mating. Males may fight quite fiercely if competing for a prospective mate, clubbing each other with their horns as well as indulging in ritualized neck wrestling.

The well-developed calf is born after a gestation period of 421–457 days and starts suckling when it is about six hours old. At birth, the youngster has different proportions than an adult okapi—its head is relatively small, its neck short, and its legs thicker and longer. It

CALVING GROUNDS

In some areas, specifically in the Serengeti, female giraffes return year after year to traditional calving grounds, usually situated within the core area of an original home range. Even if the cow has since wandered farther afield, it may still return to this same spot to calve. These sites do not share any common features that mark them out as suitable places for birth to occur—one cow may favor open parkland while another seeks greater shelter in more dense vegetation.

It is not known whether the okapi shares the habit of returning to the same calving area, but it is unlikely due to its solitary habits. The fact that a usually silent female has to call to attract a mate indicates that the bulls need some time to locate her. This is borne out by the fact that she remains in heat for a relatively long time and scent marks profusely with urine at this time.

OKAPI CALVES *suckle from their mother until they are nearly ten months old.*

Illustration Robin Budden/Wildlife Art Agency

A dominant male giraffe (below) *will mate with as many females as he can.*

Nicholas/ZEFA

ⓘⓝ S I G H T

GIRAFFE CRECHES

When a calf reaches three to four weeks old, its mother usually shepherds it into the company of other youngsters in the group to form a sort of crèche. Although this frees the mothers to wander a little farther afield to browse, the group is always watched over by a couple of females—the mothers taking turns.

Where before this time a cow rarely wanders farther than 80 ft (25 m) away from her calf, she is now able to wander as far away as 656 ft (200 m). She returns to her calf at nightfall to suckle it, remaining with it through the night. During the first week of its life it usually suckles once an hour; after two weeks this drops to once every three hours, and from then on it gets less frequent. Youngsters begin to wander with the herd from about six months old.

also has a conspicuous mane. The calf generally stays hidden for the first two weeks of life, guarded closely by its mother, or possibly another cow with a calf in the same area. The cow and calf maintain contact by calling to each other. The calf is weaned at eight to ten months, and although the male reaches sexual maturity at four years old—the female a year earlier—neither sex is fully grown or developed until nearer five years old. Horns begin to grow on the male when he reaches a year old. ∎

LIFE CYCLE

Giraffes are able to breed at any time. In some places, however, conception appears to take place during the rainy season so that birth occurs in the dry months. In the Serengeti, most births take place from May to August. Cows reach sexual maturity at about three and a half—bulls a year later—but giraffes generally do not breed until they are four and a half and seven or eight respectively. Females can go on producing young until they are at least twenty years old.

RITUALIZED COURTSHIP

Quite frequently a younger bull in an area will consort with a female approaching estrus, indulging in initial courtship behavior; however, it is usually the dominant bull within the core of the range that actually mates with her. The dominant bull spends much of his time wandering the area looking for receptive females. He inspects each one by licking her tail, which encourages her to urinate. The urine runs over his lips and he responds by curling his upper lip upward—an action known as the

A mother encouraging her newborn to stand in the Masai Mara, Kenya (below).

Jonathan Scott/Planet Earth Pictures

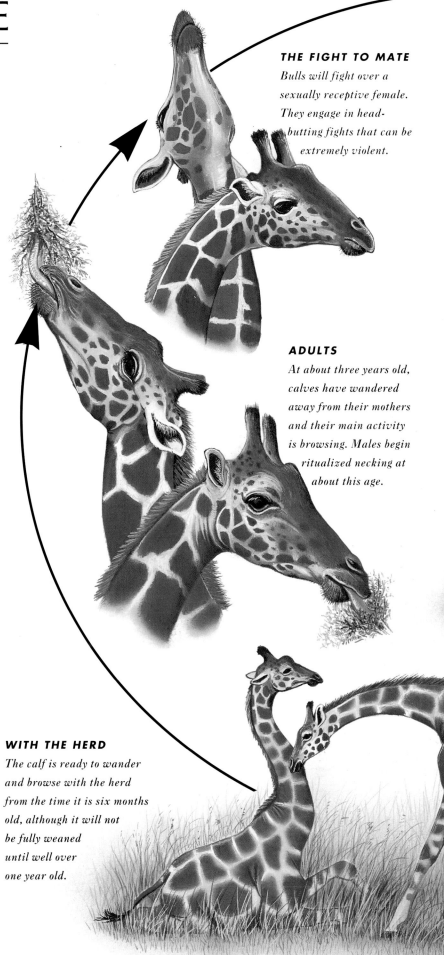

THE FIGHT TO MATE
Bulls will fight over a sexually receptive female. They engage in head-butting fights that can be extremely violent.

ADULTS
At about three years old, calves have wandered away from their mothers and their main activity is browsing. Males begin ritualized necking at about this age.

WITH THE HERD
The calf is ready to wander and browse with the herd from the time it is six months old, although it will not be fully weaned until well over one year old.

BIRTH

A cow gives birth to her calf standing up, the calf dropping some 6.5 ft (2 m) to the ground. It will be up on its feet and suckling within one hour.

CRECHE

When the calf is a month or so old, the cow moves it into the company of other calves. The young are constantly guarded by one or two cows, while the others browse.

All illustrations Kim Thompson

flehmen reaction. Testing the urine probably helps him to gauge her sexual receptivity; additional courtship behavior involves him nudging her gently with his muzzle or horns, or trying to rest his neck on her back. If she is ready for mating he will slide his forelegs onto her flanks and mount her.

Giraffes have a long gestation—approximately 457 days—so cows give birth at intervals of about twenty to thirty months (the minimum recorded time is sixteen months). Usually just one calf is born, but twins are not unknown.

The female gives birth standing up, so the newborn calf has to drop to the ground. Well developed at birth, it appears to suffer no harm and is up on its wobbly legs within about 15 minutes. The 6-ft- (1.8-m-) tall calf will take its first drink within an hour.

A YOUNG GIRAFFE CAN OUTRUN A LION BUT IT GENERALLY LACKS THE STAMINA TO OUTRUN A HYENA

For the first week or so of its life, the cow keeps her calf in isolation, watching over it with a fiercely protective, maternal devotion. At this time, she never moves far from her calf, so it is always in her sight, usually lying by a bush or tree, half-hidden by the grass. If the calf is alarmed it lowers its head almost to ground level, and the markings on its coat, already present at birth, afford it almost complete camouflage. When it is three to four weeks old, the cow moves it to the company of other youngsters in a guarded crèche.

Cows are fierce in the protection of their young, although the initial line of defense is concealment—one reason why calves spend much of their time lying down in the long grass. ∎

FROM BIRTH TO DEATH

GIRAFFE

GESTATION: 400–468 DAYS	**WEANED/FEMALES:** 12–16 MONTHS
NUMBER OF YOUNG: 1	
HEIGHT AT BIRTH: 5–6.2 FT (165–190 CM) AT SHOULDER	**SEXUAL MATURITY/MALES:** 4–5 YEARS
WEIGHT AT BIRTH: 103–154 LB (47–70 KG)	**SEXUAL MATURITY/FEMALES:** 3–4 YEARS (USUALLY DO NOT BREED FOR AT LEAST ANOTHER YEAR)
FIRST SUCKLES: WITHIN 1 HOUR	
WEANED/MALES: 12–14 MONTHS	**LONGEVITY:** 26 YEARS

OKAPI

GESTATION: 421–457 DAYS	**SEXUAL MATURITY/MALES:** 4 YEARS
NUMBER OF YOUNG: 1	
HEIGHT AT BIRTH: 2.2–2.7 FT (72–83 CM) AT SHOULDER	**SEXUAL MATURITY/FEMALES:** 3 YEARS
WEIGHT AT BIRTH: 35 LB (16 KG)	**LONGEVITY IN WILD:** NOT KNOWN (33 YEARS IN CAPTIVITY)
WEANED: 8–10 MONTHS	

PEACEABLE VICTIMS

HUMAN FASCINATION WITH THIS GENTLE GIANT OF THE AFRICAN GRASSLANDS HAS INEVITABLY LED TO A SERIOUS REDUCTION IN ITS NUMBERS OVER THE CENTURIES

T he statuesque giraffe has fascinated man since earliest times. The Ptolemies—successors of the Pharaohs—kept famed menageries in Alexandria, and Ptolemy II, King of Egypt around 285–247 B.C., kept a giraffe. Julius Caesar brought some giraffes to Rome, possibly to help celebrate his victories in Africa and perhaps also as a gift for Cleopatra. The poet Horace claimed them to be a cross between a camel and a leopard. The Romans hoped that this strange beast would prove as ferocious as it was huge, thus providing a new adversary in the Coliseum. In this they were deeply disappointed, and the elder Pliny (A.D. 23–79)—a naturalist, encyclopedist, and writer—described it as being

Nick Greaves/Planet Earth Pictures

THE 15TH-CENTURY CHINESE REVERED THE GIRAFFE AS AN EMBLEM OF PERFECT PEACE, HARMONY, AND VIRTUE

Bushman rock paintings (above) *in Inange Cave, Zimbabwe, show hunters and giraffe.*

This giraffe (right) was *killed by a truck on the outskirts of Nairobi, Kenya.*

"more remarkable for appearance than ferocity." The first—and possibly only—slaughter of a giraffe in the arena is recorded occurring in A.D. 180.

In Renaissance Florence, Lorenzo the Magnificent imported a giraffe for his beautiful gardens, and in 1414 one was sent from Malindi in Kenya to a Chinese emperor, again no doubt as a status symbol. Received in the Great Hall of Receptions, it caused a sensation, but later came to be held sacred. All of the early explorers to Africa— including Livingstone—wrote about the giraffe. The first giraffe to be exhibited in America arrived at the Central Park Zoo in New York City in 1827.

PRIZE QUARRY OF THE HUNTERS

Inevitably, human association with the giraffe has not been one of only fascinated observation. Rock paintings and engravings of the Sahara Desert

from thousands of years ago show giraffes being shot with arrows, attacked with spears, or trapped in snares. Such hunting has continued throughout the centuries. Native Africans have long killed giraffes using the kind of snares depicted in those early rock paintings—a wooden circle with sharp, inward-pointing spokes that overlapped at the center. This was tied to a heavy log with a long, tough rope, placed over a hole in the ground, and then camouflaged with earth and vegetation. A giraffe stepping on this would be held firm and helpless.

Tribespeople of the Sudan, Chad, and southern Ethiopia traditionally hunted giraffes from horseback, galloping after them, brandishing long swords or lances. A giraffe killed in this way was

William S. Paton/Bruce Coleman Ltd.

This chart shows the former and present distribution of the giraffe.

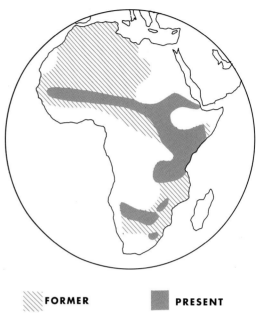

▨ FORMER   ▨ PRESENT

Human persecution has undoubtedly threatened the giraffe's continuing survival, but long before it was killed in vast numbers, it had become absent from much of its former range. In prehistoric times, species of giraffes were widespread in Europe and Asia, as well as throughout most of Africa. Climatic changes through prehistoric eras changed the grasslands of these areas, frequently into deserts—a habitat in which a giraffe has no hope of survival. It is thought that giraffes disappeared from Egypt in about 2600 B.C., but survived in Morocco until about A.D. 600.

During the 20th century, the changes to the giraffe's habitat have been caused by humans, not by climate. As a result of these changes, the relentless hunting, and epidemics of rinderpest—a usually fatal infectious viral disease that affects cattle—within the last 100 years, giraffes have disappeared from most of western and southern Africa and are becoming increasingly confined in East Africa. Where, at the beginning of the century, they were found widely and continuously in savanna country south of the Sahara, they are now found only in scattered and isolated populations.

ALONGSIDE MAN

In the late 1970s there remained only 180 or so Rothschild's giraffes in their native Rift Valley of Kenya. Time was running out for this subspecies, as its range was fast being turned into small farms. Jack and Betty Leslie Melville were a Nairobi couple who decided to act. Setting out on horseback, they captured a young cow, which they named Daisy. She was joined shortly by Marlon, a three-week-old bull. The captives were ferried more than 200 miles (320 km) to their new home in Nairobi—by minibus! Their story is told in the Leslie Melvilles' enchanting book *Raising Daisy Rothschild*, which also gives a valuable insight into the nature of these peaceable animals.

Hutchison Library

revered—and so was a horse that could keep up with it. There was no higher recommendation for a horse by the Sudanese Arabs than to say it could overtake a giraffe, and if one was able to do so twice in a day, it was declared "fit for a king." Such a hunt was considered a thrilling adventure, and as many pursued giraffes—if not more—remained free as were actually killed. It was a dangerous pursuit for a man and successful giraffe hunters were greatly respected and long remembered.

A visitor and giraffe (above) greet each other in one of Nairobi's private parks.

GIRAFFES AND OKAPIS IN DANGER

THE MOST COMMON SUBSPECIES IN THE SERENGETI IS THE MASAI GIRAFFE. THE RETICULATED GIRAFFE—FOUND MOST FREQUENTLY IN NORTHERN KENYA—IS OVERALL ONE OF THE MOST COMMON OF THE SUBSPECIES AND MAY STILL BE FOUND IN THE WILD OUTSIDE PARKS AND RESERVES.

NEITHER THE GIRAFFE NOR THE OKAPI IS LISTED BY THE INTERNATIONAL UNION FOR THE CONSERVATION OF NATURE (IUCN) IN THEIR *RED DATA BOOK* OF ENDANGERED ANIMALS. HOWEVER, THE FOLLOWING THREATS STILL REMAIN:

GIRAFFE:

POACHING, HUNTING	FOR SKIN, MEAT, AND TAIL
HABITAT DESTRUCTION	TREE CLEARANCE FOR COOKING FUEL, SOIL EROSION RESULTING FROM GRAZING BY DOMESTIC LIVESTOCK

OKAPI:

POACHING	IN MORE REMOTE FORESTED AREAS

Traditional hunting methods by native people did not threaten the giraffe, but when foreigners began to settle in Africa, the giraffe's plight became increasingly more desperate. Not only did they massacre the gentle animal themselves, but they also equipped native hunters with far more efficient weapons—firearms—against which no animal has even a sporting chance. Between the two world wars, giraffes were slaughtered at an unprecedented rate.

The killing was undoubtedly done in the name of "sport" or simply because the animals were there. Some farmers claimed giraffes were a threat to their corn and other crops, as well as to their fences, although given the choice between any crop and an acacia bush, a giraffe would always go for the acacia. Giraffes have been killed for their meat, which is tough but is said to have a good flavor. They were also valued for their hides; the incredibly thick skin—about an inch (2.5 cm) thick—can be fashioned into buckets to make excellent water carriers. Foreigners used it further to make reins and traces (long straps for harnesses), as well as whips and other items. Native people used the strong sinews to make bowstrings and traditional musical instruments, while the hide made an effective covering for their shields.

Some African tribes attributed magical properties to the giraffe's tail, which would be used as badges of high office by chiefs. The hairs on the tip were made into bracelets, which later became prized tourist items, and there are recent reports of giraffes being killed simply for their tail tassels. Once this had been cut off, the carcass would be left on the grasslands as an unexpected meal for scavenging vultures and hyenas. ∎

Nicholas Parfitt/Tony Stone Worldwide

INTO THE FUTURE

Absent from much of its former range (see Then and Now, p. 831), the giraffe is now a protected species. However, it survives principally in reserves, national parks, and zoos, and its future outside of these areas is far from certain. In addition to its natural predators—chiefly lions and hyenas—it suffers at the hands of poachers, whether for its meat or for the tail hairs used in bracelets. The solution to poaching must be, as in the case of so many big game species, to provide more funds for those policing the reserves. Tourists should also be dissuaded from supporting the trophy trade, which in turn will reduce the market value of animal products, making poaching less lucrative.

Park and reserve management must, furthermore, address the problem of habitat degradation. Local inhabitants take the savanna trees for cooking fuel. This is largely unnecessary, as special acacia and eucalyptus plantations could yield a sustainable

PREDICTION

SUBSPECIES IN THE WILD

The giraffe can adapt to human presence and breeds well in captivity. Poaching and habitat loss, however, if left unchecked, will reduce numbers in the wild, threatening the survival of isolated subspecies no longer able to interbreed.

fuel resource and leave the wild growth for the giraffes to eat.

Sheep and cattle are unselective feeders and therefore upset the naturally balanced supply of vegetation to herbivores. The problem is compounded in areas where elephants have torn down mature trees and fires have razed fresh growth before it takes hold. Giraffes, too, take their toll on the taller trees, but do not kill them outright—fire is the chief culprit here and must be controlled.

The outlook is not all bleak: The giraffe population in the Serengeti is actually increasing at about five to six percent each year. This is in spite of a fairly high mortality rate, estimated to be some 58 percent in the first year, dropping to 8 percent in the second and third years. Ironically, however, it is high-density zones such as the Serengeti that need the most urgent attention, since the sheer mass of the various herbivores—giraffes included—could threaten their long-term survival. ∎

FARMING THE GIRAFFE

Giraffe meat has proved to be palatable—tasty, if tough—and some people foresee it as a valuable source of animal protein for humans in certain areas. Unlike many grazers, the browsing giraffe does not compete with traditional domestic livestock, living as it does on a different diet, and one that is also generally more nutritious. There are areas where the sheep and goats raised by tribespeople as a source of food have so overgrazed the available land that problems of erosion have resulted. Foliage of tall trees, on the other hand, remains relatively unexploited. The theory is that giraffes could be transferred to these areas to feed on the available mature foliage, and would then be "farmed" in the same way, in conjunction with other livestock.

THE FATE OF THE OKAPI

Like the giraffe, the okapi once had a far wider distribution than today. At one time it was found in Uganda as well as Zaire, but it has long since disappeared from the former. Before foreigners, its greatest adversaries were the pygmy tribes who share its forest homeland and have long since hunted it for its meat—probably their staple food. It was actually the pygmies who gave this animal the name okapi. The hunting by natives was unlikely to endanger the animal, but the foreigners' more wholesale slaughter, combined with destruction of its habitat, has increased the threat. The okapi has been protected by government decree since 1933, but the denseness of its homeland makes this hard to enforce, and it is known to be the victim of poachers.

Illustration Steve Kingston

GOATS

RELATIONS

Goats and sheep form the mammal subfamily Caprinae within the family Bovidae. Other bovids include:

WILD CATTLE

FOREST DUIKERS

BUSH DUIKERS

GRAZING ANTELOPES

DWARF ANTELOPES

GAZELLES

William S. Paton/Planet Earth Pictures

GOATS AND SHEEP

SEPARATING THE SHEEP FROM THE GOATS HAS NEVER BEEN MORE COMPLICATED: THE MEMBERS OF THE CAPRINAE ARE A POTENT MIXTURE OF BOTH, WITH A LITTLE ANTELOPE THROWN IN FOR GOOD MEASURE!

Four hooves land on the narrow mountain ledge, only to spring off an instant later, finding purchase on an even slimmer rocky shelf. Then the female chamois bounds gracefully over the rocky field. There she pauses, secure that she has eluded the pair of wolves stranded in the valley below. The movement of the nimble chamois is exhilarating—but no less astounding is the fact that her five-day-old kid has kept up with her leap for leap.

The chamois is a native of the highest mountains of Europe and western Asia. Surprisingly, it belongs to the Bovidae, the same family as cattle. Bovids are mainly grazers; they are also distinguished by horns with a permanent keratin covering over a bony core. The chamois is part of a bovid subfamily known as Caprinae. This subfamily includes many forms of goats, sheep, and their "goat antelope" relatives. The graceful movements of the chamois, and other high-altitude goat antelope, explain the "antelope"

Goats and sheep are artiodactyls, or mammals with an even number of toes on each foot. Like other members of the Bovidae (cattle) family, they have been domesticated for thousands of years. The Caprinae subfamily includes an interesting variety of species.

ORDER

Artiodactyla (even-toed ungulates)

SUBORDER

Ruminantia (ruminants)

FAMILY

Bovidae (horned grazers)

SUBFAMILY

Caprinae (goat antelope)

TRIBES

four

GENERA

thirteen

SPECIES

twenty-six

835

element of the subfamily's common name.

The Caprinae comprise a bewildering range of body types, sizes, and coloration. The largest is the musk ox, native to northern North America and Greenland. Its huge size and stocky build led many early observers to classify it with wild cattle, but in fact the musk ox represents one end of an evolutionary chain stretching back some 35 million years. It is, of course, a far cry from the first caprines that evolved in the humid tropical forests. The modern serows of Southeast Asia resemble these earliest caprines, probably because the habitat resembles their tropical origins.

The early members of the Caprinae subfamily already showed some signs of specialization, as they were a branch of ungulates (hoofed herbivores) that had reduced the number of digits on each foot. Remaining digits became fitted to certain tasks. This evolutionary process of digit reduction was itself divided, with some ungulates retaining an odd-numbered amount of digits (perissodactyls) and others keeping an even-numbered amount (artiodactyls). The Caprinae were part of the artiodactyls,

The saiga's curious "Roman" nose takes the harsh, icy edge off cold air as it is inhaled (above).

E. van Nostrand/Frank Lane Picture Agency

Robert Maier/Aquila

STAYING ALIVE

Originally all Caprinae were "resource defenders," occupying small areas of productive habitats. Resource defenders remain within this area for the whole year, ensuring that their nutritional needs are met and that interlopers can be fended off with fiercely aggressive behavior. That strategy developed in the ancestral home of the goat antelope, the humid tropics. It is still employed by the serow of Southeast Asia, whose habitat resembles the original home of goat antelopes. The serow itself resembles many early caprines, with its small build and selective food habits.

Animals that broke away from this early habitat had to find ways to adjust to the open landscapes of the grasslands. They evolved larger teeth and other dental changes to cope with difficult forage. Solitary defense was futile on the plains, so herds provided safety in numbers. Instead of short but effective horns, these plains herders evolved elaborate, curving horns that owe more to social hierarchy than to any real defensive purpose.

with two digits remaining on each hoof.

The extraordinary agility of the modern chamois is due in large part to this specializing. The chamois relies on its ability to find a foothold on thin rocky ledges, which are often covered in ice or snow. The main toe has a thin outer ridge that grips the rock, while a rubbery inner pad guards against slipping. The toe itself can be splayed—snowshoe-style—on slippery surfaces, or closed for gripping narrow ledges. The smaller, upper toe can act as an anchor on steep perches.

THE GRASSLAND ADVANTAGE

Gradual foot modification played a part in the species radiation of the Caprinae. Vast new grasslands were opening up about five million years ago. These new and larger territories called for speed to escape the fast predators that were developing at the same time. Greater range led to more social behavior and, with it, new defensive strategies and elaborate group structures. Body size increased and, once past the 44 lb (20 kg) threshold, led to the emergence of the now familiar horn shapes.

The magnificent ibex has been rescued from the brink of extinction through captive breeding.

THE BOVIDS' FAMILY TREE

The Bovidae family is divided into six subfamilies. The Caprinae, the goat antelope subfamily, contains twenty-six species, but is commonly divided initially into four main tribes. Common factors within tribes include horn size and shape, types of glands, skeletal shape, and behavior.

Caprines had an internal advantage that also aided their advance into new habitats. As ruminants, they had multicavity stomachs to process tough, fibrous foods. Grasslands are not welcoming for animals that are unable to break down the cellulose in plant cell walls. Already established as adaptable grazers, goat antelope capitalized on the sweeping geographical changes produced by the last ice ages. Two key factors in this success were their mobility and an ability to cooperate as a herd, with a type of collective survival instinct. They were among the first—and in some places the only—grazing mammals to colonize inhospitable environments such as baking deserts, arctic tundra, alpine plateaus, and the steep cliffs of glacial valleys.

There is no single adaptation that suits such a range of habitats, which explains the rich variety among the 26 present-day species. Perhaps the key aspect of the caprines is the range of body size and shape. Many are surefooted "mountaineers," able to escape from predators with quick-reflexed leaps. Some, such as the serow, live a solitary life. Others, such as the saiga and chamois, are social—a quality that has helped populations reestablish themselves after persecution by humans. ■

MUSK OX
Ovibos moschatus

(O-vee-boss mos-CAH-tus)

The Ovibovini tribe contains the musk ox, which is the largest goat antelope species, weighing up to 770 lb (350 kg) in the wild. Its massive build and thick fur have helped it adapt to the freezing climate of its arctic habitat.

SAIGA

Saiga tatarica

(SIE-ga tah-TAR-icka)

The saiga is native to the steppes of southern Russia and central Asia. It is reappearing in large numbers after centuries of brutal slaughter. Its tribe, the Saigini (sigh-GEE-nee), is sometimes classified with the gazelle subfamily. The Saigini tribe also contains the chiru of Tibet, China, and northern India.

SUBFAMILY
CAPRINAE
(GOATS AND SHEEP)

WILD
CATTLE

FAMILY
BOVIDAE

EVEN-TOED
UNGULATES

B/W illustrations Ruth Grewcock

SHEEP AND GOATS

Caprini

(ka-PREE-nee)

The Caprini contains the domestic sheep and goats, as well as their ancestors and other related species. Its members observe a strict hierarchy among males, with combat common.

OTHER SPECIES:

HIMALAYAN TAHR, NILGIRI TAHR, ARABIAN TAHR, BARBARY SHEEP, BLUE SHEEP, WILD GOAT, SPANISH GOAT, IBEX, MARKHOR, EAST CAUCASIAN TUR, WEST CAUCASIAN TUR, URIAL, ARGALI, MOUFLON, SNOW SHEEP, THINHORN SHEEP, AMERICAN BIGHORN SHEEP

Color illustrations Steve Kingston

CHAMOIS

Rupicapra rupicapra

(roo-pee-CAP-ra roo-pee-CAP-ra)

The chamois is a striking example of the tribe Rupicaprini *(roo-pee-ca-PREE-nee)*, whose members have evolved least from the original caprine ancestors. Like the chamois, most members of this tribe are suited to life on steep slopes.

OTHER SPECIES:

MAINLAND SEROW
JAPANESE SEROW
GORAL
MOUNTAIN GOAT

DUIKERS

GRAZING ANTELOPES

GAZELLES

ANATOMY:
THE IBEX

THE HORNS

are the showpieces of the male ibex. Extravagantly long, they are used in ceremonial combat with other males, usually during the breeding season. Those of the female are far shorter and lack the frontal ridges.

Goat antelope range in size from the Arabian tahr (above right), which often measures less than 40 in (100 cm) from head to tail, to the musk ox (above left), which can reach a length of almost 8 ft (240 cm).

DEWCLAW RAISED

Caprines are even-toed ungulates, a reference to the number of digits on each foot. Evolutionary reduction in the number of toes has left only two—the third and fourth—comprising a "cloven hoof." Many, such as the ibex, retain toes at the back of the foot called dewclaws. On level, easy terrain, the ibex holds its dewclaws aloft, but on slippery slopes it drops these natural crampons to the ground for extra grip.

DEWCLAW LOWERED

DEWCLAW

THE BEARD

may be barely noticeable in the Alpine ibex; it rarely grows longer than 2.5–3 in (6–7 cm). In the Ethiopian ibex, however, the beard may be more than twice this length.

FORELEGS

Like the hind legs, these are sturdy enough to absorb the repeated shocks sustained on the rocky crags. Permanent knee calluses are a feature of many caprines.

SKELETON
Strong leg bones support a stout, stocky body. Surefootedness and a low center of gravity combine to give the ibex an advantage in its mountain habitat.

HOOVES
The second and fifth digits of the hooves are made of rough, rounded horns that are detached from the cannon bone at the base of the leg. "Shod" with rubbery soles, these dewclaws help the ibex gain footholds on steep mountain slopes.

stout neck

sturdy legs

short tail

FOREFOOT

HIND FOOT

tibia

cannon bone

dewclaw

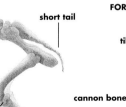

MARKHOR SAIGA BIGHORN

Horns vary widely among caprines. Resource defenders such as gorals, serows, and saigas have short, sharp horns for piercing attackers. Females usually have similar horns. Elaborate display horns such as those of the markhor or argalis are designed more for dominance rituals between males, although those of the American bighorn can inflict fatal injuries. Female bighorns have very short horns.

CLASSIFICATION

GENUS: *CAPRA*

SPECIES: *IBEX*

SIZE

HEAD-BODY LENGTH: 2.5–5.6 FT (75–170 CM)

TAIL LENGTH: 6–11.5 IN (15–29 CM)

SHOULDER HEIGHT: 2.3–3.1 FT (70–94 CM)

WEIGHT: 88–264 LB (40–120 KG)

WEIGHT AT BIRTH: 4.4–7.7 LB (2–3.5 KG)

HORN LENGTH/MALE: 40 IN (100 CM)

HORN LENGTH/FEMALE: 14 IN (35 CM)

THE MALE IS MARKEDLY LARGER THAN THE FEMALE

COLORATION

FEMALES AND VERY YOUNG MALES ARE A MID-OCHRE-BROWN. IN SUMMER, ADULT MALES ARE AN OCHRE-TAN OVERALL WITH PALER NECK, FOREHEAD, AND FLANKS, DARK LEGS, AND WHITE BELLY AND TAIL

IN LATE SUMMER, ADOLESCENT MALES DARKEN, WHILE OLDER MALES TURN GRAY

THE COAT FADES DURING WINTER, REPLACED WITH A NEW "SUMMER" GROWTH IN SPRING

FEATURES

STOCKY BODY

BROAD HOOVES WITH RUBBERY SOLES

HORNS OF MALE ARE SCIMITAR-SHAPED AND LONG; FEMALE HAS SMALLER, THINNER HORNS

SHORT BEARD IN MALE ONLY

THE COAT,

like the horns, is more spectacular in the male. It is molted in spring and replaced each year. In autumn and winter, the coat is thickened with extra woolly underhairs and long guard hairs.

THE LIMBS

of all caprid mountain goats are characteristically sturdy and powerful. The typical "mountaineering" technique involves thrusting strongly from one rock face to the other, relying on the keen edges of the hooves to find a grip. During the breeding season, rival male ibex rear up on their hind legs in display.

IBEX SKULL

smooth molars

TEETH
The array of teeth sheds light on the feeding habits of wild goats, and of most goat antelope. The upper canines are absent and molar surfaces are smooth, indicating a diet weighted predominantly toward tough, fibrous plant material.

upper canines absent

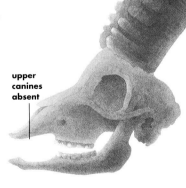

HORNS
Male wild goats have much longer horns than females. These horns are curved sharply backward, with sharp edges to the front. Ridges commonly form on the horns, appearing at irregular intervals. Horns differ from antlers in that they have a permanent bony core encased in a hardened sheath, whereas antlers are fully shed.

LONERS AND HERDERS

MOST CAPRINES EITHER FLOCK TOGETHER FOR SAFETY OR SEEK SOLITUDE BESIDE SHEER ROCK FACES. BUT AS IN ANY GROUP, THERE ARE ALSO SPECIES THAT DEFY SUCH GENERALIZATIONS

The history of caprines is one of a great march northward and outward, radiating away from tropical origins near the equator. This march involved a number of behavioral changes, none more fundamental than the change from resource defense to gregarious feeding.

These feeding patterns, which led to the wide range of caprine behavior and social structures, are themselves responses to habitat. Resource defense is the obvious way to survive in a habitat that is nutritionally rich. Individual territories need not be large, but must be assiduously patrolled to guard against others of the same species or dangerous predators. Members of the Rupicaprini tribe adopt this type of behavior, which echoes that of the original members of the subfamily.

Gregarious grazing in herds was the answer to life in the open grasslands as members of the Caprinae began to explore new habitats. Herds of saiga, which still roam the steppes of southern Russia and central Asia, provide a striking contrast to solitary species such as the serow of Southeast Asia.

SURVIVAL STRATEGIES

Interestingly, some members of the subfamily adopted radically different behavioral approaches to life in similar environments. The two approaches account for the separate development of goats and sheep. Goats developed a way of fleeing from predators that involved nimble escape, a variation of the resource defender's response. That escape strategy meant that goats developed most successfully for life on cliffs and in precipitous valleys, where they could outmaneuver less agile predators. Sheep, on the other hand, took to the herd response to predators. Clumping together, and deriving strength from numbers, meant that sheep chose the more open, rolling land near the cliffs.

These diverging behaviors led to some of the most notable developments among goat antelope, particularly among gregarious sheep. Horns, which had lost their role as defensive weapons and had become props in mating rituals, became larger and more elaborate. Social hierarchies became closely tied to these trophies.

Two North American species, the mountain goat and the American bighorn, illustrate typical ' sheep" and "goat" responses to an identical environment—the Rocky Mountains. The mountain goat has a more solitary lifestyle: It is a resource defender that patrols its cliff territory fiercely when food supplies become scarce. The bighorn, as its name implies, has a lifestyle symbolized by its large, curving horns. At breeding time, rival males engage in lengthy, ritualized combat, and the social structure of the herd is important. Unlike the mountain

Musk oxen live in herds, settling rivalry disputes with hard-hitting horn clashes (above).

C. C. Lockwood/Bruce Coleman Ltd.

John Johnson/Oxford Scientific Films

DEADLY WEAPONS

Horns are a distinguishing feature of most goat antelope, yet there is a fundamental paradox about the length of these horns: The longest and most dramatic are the least effective as defensive weapons.

Caprines with the shortest horns are primarily resource defenders. Their horns are strong, straight, sharp, and exceedingly deadly. Goral and serow horns, although effective weapons, rarely exceed 8 in (20 cm) in length.

Nimble escape and herd protection are the natural defenses of more social species; horns are used largely in ritual mating displays between males. Their length—more than 55 in (140 cm) in species such as the ibex, markhor, and argali—is impressive and plays an important part in settling mating disputes. But in terms of wounding power, these horns are like ceremonial broadswords compared with the lethal stilettos of shorter horns.

goat, the bighorn responds to food shortages by migrating seasonally to seek out new supplies.

Musk oxen, which thrive farther north than nearly any other mammal, also fit the pattern of social grazing. They appear at first to be ponderous and clumsy. With their huge form and sweeping horns, they also appear to be close relatives of cattle—hence the name. Closer examination, however, proves these to be misconceptions. They are sure-footed and nimble, able to reach a gallop of 25 mph (40 km/h). Their anatomical and chromosomal structures place them firmly in the Caprinae subfamily, making them closer relatives of domestic goats than domestic cattle.

Herds of up to a hundred musk oxen seek out moist habitats in the summer, preferring valleys, damp meadows, and shores of lakes. In the winter they move to windswept hilltops and plateaus, where most of the snow cover has been blown away.

The sometimes perplexing array of original body types and strategies has led to confusion and some disagreement about classification over the years. The Asian takin is a good example. Two of its common names—"cattle chamois" and "gnu goat"—are at odds with each other. Between them they link the takin with four different browsing mammals! ■

The Dall sheep is a relative of the American bighorn. It is found on the icy cliffs of Alaska and Canada.

HABITATS

James H. Robinson

The mountain goat's "leg warmers" stop just below the knee, allowing it to find its footing more easily.

Caprines inhabit nearly every environmental niche north of the equator. Fossils indicate that the subfamily moved slowly northward from its original tropical home. Over the same time, a number of evolutionary adaptations were made, dictated by climate and environment. Those adaptations are at their most extreme for the northernmost members of the subfamily, the musk ox of North America and the takin of Asia: These are the giants of the Caprinae.

The Caprinae subfamily is characterized by the diversity of its 26 species—a natural result of their pattern of expansion into a wide range of habitats, many of which are extreme and inhospitable. The earliest goat antelope were resource defenders in a humid tropical climate. In habitat and appearance they resembled the modern serows of Asia. Other members of the serow's tribe, the Rupicaprini, share its resource-defense social strategy. But these relatives—the goral of the Himalayas, the North American mountain goat, and the European chamois—have evolved into very different forms.

LIFE IN THE MOUNTAINS

The goral, although closely related to the serow, is adapted to a more mountainous habitat. It gleans its diet of twigs, grass, and nuts on rugged terrain at altitudes of 3,300–13,200 ft (1,000–4,000 m). Its long, stout legs are well suited to climbing.

The mountain goat is a native of the Rocky Mountains. Its short horns, a trait shared with serows and gorals, indicate the attacking strategy of a typical resource defender. The mountain goat

in SIGHT

DEALING WITH PREDATORS

Goat antelope display a range of responses to predators. These actions are partly dictated by environment and partly by their evolutionary adaptations; although, as is often the case within the subfamily, these two factors are intertwined.

The most sedentary resource defenders such as Asian serows must rely on themselves to take the bull by the horns—quite literally. Their short horns enable them to take on, or at least warn off, animals as fierce as the Asian brown bear.

More gregarious animals such as sheep adopt the strategy of safety in numbers. Their instinct is to run into the flock and clump together. Surefooted species such as wild goats and chamois put space between themselves and predators. Few attackers can pursue these animals up the apparently sheer rock faces that provide their escape routes.

One of the most formidable in conflict is surely the musk ox, whose herd draws together as a defense against the main enemies—wolves and polar bears. The herd members head as one for a patch of high ground, then bunch together and form a chain, facing outward toward the attackers. If surrounded, they will form a living stockade, within which young animals are protected. Individual bulls and cows break free of the chain and challenge the attackers until they withdraw.

DISTRIBUTION

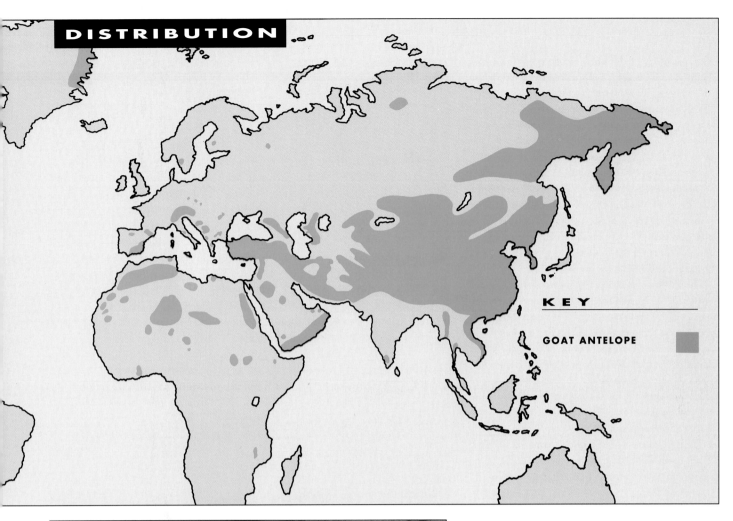

KEY

GOAT ANTELOPE

seeks out inaccessible, often snow-covered rocky terrain, which explains its thick, white coat. But the mountain goat has another feature—"pantaloons" on its legs—that shows even further adaptation to its environment. These woolen leggings stop at about the knee, so the lower legs have more sensitivity for finding purchase on narrow ledges. The mountain goat is a renowned climber, able to climb more than 1,470 ft (450 m) in about twenty minutes.

The chamois is an example of resource defense beginning to give way to a more sociable strategy. It has the same climbing skills as the mountain goat, combined with an agility and fleetness of foot that serve it in defense. The longer horns of the chamois, starting to outgrow their purpose as lethal blades, are gradually turning into sparring equipment, indicating a move toward a more herd-oriented lifestyle.

The "longhorn" species that many people associate with the goat antelope—species such as the ibex, urial, markhor, and American bighorn—gained their distinctive look by adopting mating strategies that themselves were a response to environment. Grouping together in herds, at least seasonally, these animals represent a more evolved social pattern.

With exquisite poise, an ibex rears up in a rivalry challenge, seeming oblivious to the chasm below.

Jean Paul Ferrero/Ardea

845

In an entirely different environment, spectacular adaptations allow the musk ox to survive the harsh arctic climate of northern Canada and Greenland. It has a dense undercoat, which neither cold nor water can penetrate. The shaggy outer coat reaches almost to the ground and protects the animal from rain and snow. Broad hooves spread the weight of the musk ox in the same way that snowshoes support people.

Another difficulty of living in the Land of the Midnight Sun presents itself in the six months or more of noontime darkness. The musk ox uses its large pupils and light-sensitive retinas to pick up enough light from the dimmest sources—the moon, the stars, and a faint glow on the horizon.

The saiga is a migratory species that has adapted successfully to its cold treeless habitat, which ranges across windswept plains from the Volga through to central Asia. Its sense of hearing has diminished in response to the landscape. On the featureless plains there is very little advantage to be gained by hearing a potential danger; spotting it on the horizon is more useful. The saiga's eyesight is correspondingly keen, and herds respond quickly to dangers seen up to 3,300 ft (1,000 m) away.

The most startling feature of the saiga is its large, convex nose, with downward-pointing nostrils. This large nasal cavity seems to be an adaptation to the

temperature extremes and the dust of its homeland. The nasal passages are lined inside with hairs, glands, and mucous tracts. In each nostril is a sac lined with mucous membranes that appear in no other animal except the whale. The enlarged snout seems to be used to warm up cold air, or moisturize dry air before it enters the respiratory system. The hairs act as effective dust filters. The bulbous snout must also account for the saiga's keen sense of smell—a necessity in an open habitat where constant updrafts waft most scents away. ∎

FOCUS ON

ABRUZZO NATIONAL PARK

Abruzzo National Park covers 154 sq miles (400 sq km) of high terrain in central Italy. It is Italy's second oldest national park, established in 1923 to protect the wildlife of the Apennines, the chain of mountains that forms the "spine" of the country. The chamois and other mountain-dwelling mammals benefit from this refuge from the shooting culture that prevails in much of Italy.

Glacial relief typifies the highest ground, particularly around the park's highest point, Monte Petroso (7,355 ft/2,247 m). The high valleys are shrouded in beech forests, parts of which date back to the last ice age. The park has Italy's highest concentration of wolves, as well as the Abruzzo brown bear, a subspecies unique to the Apennines. Other denizens include otters, badgers, pine martens, and red squirrels.

The high peaks are refuges for golden eagles. On the slopes, just above the tree line, chamois graze in the summer months. They descend in winter to feed on young pine shoots and mosses. The park is the home of Italy's 400 remaining Apennine chamois.

Paolo Fioratti/Oxford Scientific Films

TEMPERATURE AND RAINFALL

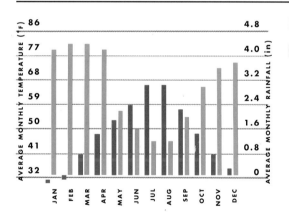

■ **TEMPERATURE**

■ **RAINFALL**

The high altitude of the park, coupled with the natural break that the Apennines form against humid winds from the west, produce a severe mountain climate. Sudden and severe snowstorms are common in winter.

NEIGHBORS

Strict prohibitions against hunting, fishing, and collecting native flora protect a wide range of wildlife within Abruzzo National Park, where conditions are often described as alpine.

GOSHAWK

LAMMERGEIER

The goshawk resembles a large sparrow hawk. It hunts in forests, preying chiefly on other birds.

The lammergeier spends hours soaring on mountain updrafts, descending only to feed on carrion.

Neighbor illustrations Peter Bull, except: goshawk Dale Evans, wildcat Ruth Grewcock

Abruzzo National Park is only about 50 miles (80 km) east of Rome, making it easy to reach from the Italian capital. But the park's high average altitude makes for a distinctly cool climate, and snow still lies deep on the Apennine slopes when Romans start seeking escape from the city's heat each year.

ABRUZZO NATIONAL PARK

Adriatic Sea

ROME

ITALY

NAPLES

Mediterranean Sea

BROWN BEAR

The nocturnal Apennine brown bear belongs to the same species as the massive grizzlies of North America.

ITALIAN LIZARD

The Italian lizard nests in crags along the Apennine rock faces, where it also suns itself during the day.

APOLLO BUTTERFLY

Apollos can soar like birds of prey on the updrafts of mountain cliffs—a rare talent among insects.

WILDCAT

The wildcat looks like a large domestic cat with a thick, ringed tail. It preys on small rodents and birds.

ALPINE CHOUGH

This mountain-dwelling member of the crow family is a skillful flier that nests in cleft rocks.

FOOD AND FEEDING

Caprines are herbivores subsisting on a diet of plant material. At their most basic level they defend localized, productive sources of food. Individual male serows, for example, inhabit about 18.5 acres (7.5 hectares) of wooded gorges and grassy slopes. This area, which becomes clearly marked out as the male's territory, is enough to satisfy all of his nutritional needs.

No other caprine species has such a clearly defined territory; however, animals such as the mountain goat and chamois remain in a restricted feeding area, the knowledge of which becomes important for the survival of future generations. In their mountain habitats, plant cover is thinner and more subject to climatic fluctuations.

The most social species are also the most migratory, capable of difficult passages over mountains or across plains in search of food. Saigas form large and mobile herds, but their constant roaming is not simply seasonal. Instead it is dictated by more pressing factors related to food supplies. Saigas will not settle long in an area likely to undergo summer droughts and prolonged deep winter snows. They seem to be collectively alert to weather changes, because they will starve if more than 8 in (20 cm) of snow covers the ground for two weeks.

Saigas have adjusted to their drought-prone habitat by being able to derive their moisture needs from green plants, not needing to locate water holes unless there are no green plants to be found. They eat primarily shrubs and herbs, turning to grass only during the spring.

CHEWING THE CUD

As ruminants, goat antelope are well equipped to digest and metabolize a wide range of plant matter. They clip the plant matter with their lower incisors—they have no upper incisors—and press it against the tongue or the gums of the upper jaw. Then they swallow it so that it passes into a special stomach chamber called the rumen.

It is there that ruminants can employ their secret digestive weapons. No mammal can produce a digestive juice to break down cellulose, the material of plant cell walls. But cultures of certain bacteria thrive inside the rumen. These bacteria attack the cellulose while the meal is churned inside the rumen for several hours. The mushy result, the cud, is then brought back up the throat. The animal can then "chew the cud," usually at its leisure, before swallowing the food a second time. This time it goes into the stomach proper to be fully digested.

This digestive advantage lies behind the subfamily's radiation into such a range of habitats—it also helps certain species reestablish themselves from positions of near extinction. Mouflon were once common throughout Europe, but were hunted extensively until well into this century. Native

VERSATILE SAIGAS

In spring, the saiga herds take advantage of the fresh, succulent grass shoots, which supply their water needs (below).

AMAZING FACTS

PERPETUAL PLAINS

How can grasslands survive beneath herds of ruminants? Or, rather, how is it that while bad farming techniques can lead to soil erosion, vast plains withstand the ceaseless munching of "unthinking" grazers?

The answer lies in the extraordinary regenerative ability of grass itself. The cellulose of its cell walls deters all but the most effective ruminants. Even then, the stems are often buried below the soil, so that grazers have access only to the leaves. Brushfires on the plains quickly sweep past the grass, burning only the old, dry leaves.

Grazers in turn provide a service to the grass. They trample and eat the seedlings of bushes or trees that would otherwise take root and rob the grasses of vital light.

populations remain only on the islands of Sardinia and Corsica, but reintroduced populations are beginning to thrive again on the mainland of Central Europe. Feeding adaptability seems to play a large part in the mouflon's success in these "new" habitats. The mouflon seems capable of eating every type of vegetation: flowers, grass, and buds and shoots of bushes and trees. It can even eat poisonous plants such as deadly nightshade with no obvious ill effects.

Herds of musk oxen support themselves in the unproductive Arctic tundra. Their preference for

FOREST FEEDER
Found mainly in the equatorial forests and rocky habitats of Asia, the serow feeds at dawn and dusk. It browses on lush plants with juicy shoots and leaves (above).

It takes more than a scattering of snow to deter a bighorn sheep from finding sustenance (above).

moist summer habitats such as river valleys and lake shores leads them to areas where enough soil has collected to support reeds and grasses. Finding food in the barren tundra seems hard enough in the summer, but winter sustenance is even more precious. The musk oxen dig craters in the snow to get at the vegetation. High-ranking males break through icy crusts that might form, using their heads like sledgehammers. Lesser-ranking males are often chased away from these craters if food is scarce. ∎

SOCIAL STRUCTURE

The evolutionary fanning out of the Caprinae subfamily into so many far-flung habitats has led to different social structures. Many of the most distinctive physiological features of caprines, such as scent-producing glands and dramatic horns, are reflections of how individual species behave.

The most primitive, solitary social patterns are displayed by resource defenders such as the serow and other species in the tribe Rupicaprini. These social patterns probably most closely resemble those of the earliest caprines.

These solitary browsers choose to meet others of their species only for breeding purposes. Males often use scent to mark out the territories that will provide their needs. Defense comes in the form of their short, sharp horns, which they use upon predators and trespassing male goats.

Social hierarchies only developed when goat antelope began to colonize the open grasslands outside their original range. The herd became the social unit that provided the best protection against predators. One-to-one encounters with predators became rare, so horns lost their original function; instead they became closely related to social structures centering on male dominance within the herd.

Ritualized combat is at the extreme end of a range of gestures used by animals that form herds. Adult male chamois are usually solitary, but during the rut they join females to form harems. Much of their time is spent warning off would-be suitors from the ranks of younger males. A series of gestures provides the "language" of these encounters. The adult male, for example, uses a side display to intimidate other males. He holds his head high, and the long hairs on his arched back stand up, making his body appear larger, as he walks stiffly toward his rival. Younger males use a similar threat gesture, but without the erect back hairs. Submissive males stretch out low and creep away, or they scamper off in the alarmed tail-up posture.

HEAD BANGERS

Few sights are more thrilling than the rivalry battles between American bighorn bucks. They collide with a shocking crash, but their brains are protected from damage by a double layer of bone, and the facial skin is especially thick to cushion the savage blows.

Few predators are foolish enough to try breaking up a defensive line of musk oxen.

Not all chamois communication is aggressive, however; their acute senses are put to the use of the herd as a whole. Many herds have been observed to post a sentinel, which, at the first sign of danger, stamps his feet and utters a shrill, high-pitched whistle. That is the cue for the herd's escape, and they can run off at speeds of up to 30 mph (50 km/h), even over rough ground.

Ibex are also native to the Alps but display an even more elaborate social structure, centered around the dominant male. Two factors signal dominance among males—horn length and body size—and older males clearly have an advantage in both areas. Moreover, the bodies of ibex males continue to grow for the first eight years.

Both ibex sexes mingle in winter, but in warmer weather adult males form their own group, leaving the does with kids and younger animals. The social hierarchy for the next mating season is decided by battles within these male-only groupings. Bucks raise themselves on their hind legs and crash their horns together as they come down heavily. ∎

Hans Reinhard/Bruce Coleman Ltd.

in SIGHT
STAKING A CLAIM

Resource-defending species of caprines are solitary by nature and guard their territories fiercely. To warn off potential territorial rivals, many species mark their territories with strong-smelling secretions. The most common scent-marking system uses secretions from the preorbital glands, located in pits inside the skull.

The serow is typical of this solitary, scent-marking group, with clearly marked territories. A group of four or five will divide a hillside, marking the perimeter of their respective territories by rubbing their heads against tree trunks, stumps, or other prominent landmarks. The scent is said to be sharp, like that of a duiker.

Preorbital glands are important for social species as well. During the December rut, a saiga buck's nose swells up and his preorbital glands release a strong-smelling secretion. This odor is enough to warn other males of his arrival. Bucks with harems will respond to the scent by chasing rivals away.

Robin Budden/Wildlife Art Agency

LIFE CYCLE

The 26 species of caprines live in a range of habitats—from the Asian jungle and the sunbaked Ethiopian highlands to the Arctic tundra. Mating strategies and individual appearance are conditioned by the surroundings, but on a more basic level, the subfamily shares a number of fundamental similarities in reproduction and life cycle.

The range of habitats, although diverse, is almost completely inhospitable or remote. This can affect the number of offspring and the life span. Litter size is usually small, a response to territories that are either productive yet strictly delineated or looser and potentially unsupportive. Three offspring is usually the maximum, but most litters have only one or two newborn; these are always well developed and precocious.

Population growth, or stability, is achieved not through endless waves of litters but through small annual increases. This is especially true where climatic conditions are extreme. It is not surprising that two species with life spans of 20 years—the musk ox and American bighorn—are natives of the Arctic tundra and rugged mountains respectively.

SOCIAL CUSTOMS

The major mating differences among goat antelope are dictated by social structure. Among the more primitive resource defenders, such as the two species of serows, the sexes look very similar; both, too, observe scent-marking behaviors. The mating season is in October and November and mating itself is preceded by an elaborate courtship. The male licks at the female's mouth, strikes between her hind legs with his forelegs, and rubs his horns against her genitalia.

The sexes differ more greatly in appearance among the more social goat antelope. Social hierarchies, often linked to horn length, dictate mating strategy. Ritual combat between high-ranking males involves head butting and prolonged clashes of horns. Dominant males in some species, such as the saiga, can even acquire harems.

SCENT FRENZY
During the rut, adult males use the scent glands at the base of their horns to mark more or less everything in sight—including each other (above).

EARLY LEARNER
The juvenile mountain goat rapidly develops in skill and confidence, and before long it is surefooted on the rocky slopes, just like its parents (left).

Stephen Message/Wildlife Art Agency

*in*SIGHT

SMELLY BILLIES

Scent marking and scent recognition play an important role in the behavior of many caprine species. This is usually the domain of the bucks, which need to establish and enforce territorial limits or to be warned of approaching rivals. The source of the distinctive scent is usually a secretion from a gland such as the preorbital gland in the skull.

Billy goats (male goats) often adopt a simpler—yet equally effective—way of advertising their presence. They simply spray themselves with urine and let the resulting body odor speak for itself.

John Daniels/Ardea

The American bighorn displays many of the "typical" behaviors of long-horned, social goat antelope. It is a native of alpine and desertlike habitats of western North America. The massive spiral horns of older males reach spectacular lengths—up to 3.75 feet (1.15 m).

During the mating season, high-ranking males of similar horn size have dramatic battles, rushing at each other and crashing their horns together fiercely. Such encounters are often protracted, and may continue for hours. Occasionally one of the animals is killed, but certain adaptations reduce the possibility of fatal wounds. A double layer of bone covers the

Like so many young ungulates, the mountain goat kid is soon mobile and keeping up with its mother.

GROWING UP

The life of an American mountain goat

QUICK START
The kid scrambles to its feet almost at once after its birth. It sticks close by its mother's side (above), bleating piteously to attract her attention in times of danger.

KIDS AT PLAY
At two weeks old, the kids are indulging in lively games, butting and leaping in mimicry of the adults (left).

brain, and skull bones are particularly hard. The neck bones, too, are tough, and form an especially strong joint with the skull. Fractured horns, however, are a common occurrence.

Although these high-ranking feuds are fierce, lower-ranking—and therefore smaller-horned—males are not excluded from the herd. Instead, they are treated as females by the dominant males, an instinctive strategy that sustains herd sizes and provides extra defense while grazing. Correspondingly, younger males are tacitly encouraged to stay with the herd in order to acquire knowledge from the older males about the best grazing areas and escape routes. These well-stocked sites are widely scattered in extensive forested regions.

The bighorn ewe produces one or two lambs in June after about a six-month gestation. The offspring are well developed and within days are able to accompany her to graze on high mountain pastures. Nevertheless, the mother maintains close links with her young, and they are fully weaned only by the time they are six months old.

By winter, ibex bucks have stopped fighting for superiority, and high-ranking males are accorded deference by those who remember the outcomes of the summer battles. The rut has two stages. In the first or common rut, all the bucks court the does by repeating a series of foreplay gestures: These include stretching out the body, pulling the head back, raising the tail, flipping the tongue, rotating the head, and swinging a foreleg forward. Lesser-ranking bucks recede in the second (individual) rut, in which the highest-ranking male courts, and mates with, most of the does. ■

FROM BIRTH TO DEATH

BIGHORN SHEEP
GESTATION: 175 DAYS
LITTER SIZE: 1
BREEDING: OCTOBER–DECEMBER
WEIGHT AT BIRTH: 8.8 LB (4 KG)
EYES OPEN: AT BIRTH
WEANING: 4–6 MONTHS
GRAZING: 3–6 DAYS
LONGEVITY: AVERAGE 9 YEARS IN WILD; 24 YEARS IN CAPTIVITY

MOUNTAIN GOAT
GESTATION: 186 DAYS
LITTER SIZE: 1, RARELY 2 OR 3
BREEDING: NOVEMBER–JANUARY
WEIGHT AT BIRTH: 7 LB (3.2 KG)
EYES OPEN: AT BIRTH
WEANING: 3 MONTHS
GRAZING: 1 WEEK
SEXUAL MATURITY: 30 MONTHS
LONGEVITY: MALE 14 YEARS, FEMALE 18 YEARS

MUSK OX
GESTATION: 8.5 MONTHS
LITTER SIZE: 1
BREEDING: JULY–SEPTEMBER
WEIGHT AT BIRTH: 18–33 LB (8–15 KG)
EYES OPEN: AT BIRTH
WEANING: 10–18 MONTHS
BROWSING: 1 WEEK
SEXUAL MATURITY: 3–4 YEARS
LONGEVITY: 20–24 YEARS

SAIGA
GESTATION: 139 DAYS
LITTER SIZE: FIRST YEAR 1, THEN 2
BREEDING: DECEMBER
WEIGHT AT BIRTH: 7.5 LB (3.4 KG)
EYES OPEN: AT BIRTH
WEANING: 3–4 MONTHS
GRAZING: 8–10 DAYS
SEXUAL MATURITY: FEMALE 8 MONTHS, MALE 20 MONTHS
LONGEVITY: 6–10 YEARS

A TALENT FOR SURVIVAL

CAPRINES WOULD SEEM TO HAVE EVOLVED WITH ALL THE QUALITIES NECESSARY FOR SUCCESS AS A GROUP; BUT, PARADOXICALLY, THEIR OWN RELATIVES ARE SOME OF THEIR GREATEST ENEMIES

The spread of the Caprinae to some of the most inhospitable habitats of the northern hemisphere indicates a distinct talent for survival. Radiating from their original range, they have established themselves in deserts, steppes, Arctic tundra, and a variety of mountain environments.

Within the subfamily were the ancestors of the domesticated goat and sheep. The subsequent patterns of behavior and appearance of these genera were conditioned by the way in which the ancestral goats and sheep adapted to habitat and to predators. The goats, with their preference for eluding predators, colonized rocky cliffs. Early sheep stayed off the cliffs, preferring to remain on grassy fields where they could flock together in the face of danger.

That early division is not surprising, and not an exceptional story in the evolution of mammals as a whole. However, the innate ability of the subfamily to adapt to surroundings has proved that these divisions are fluid. Wild species of some goats resemble sheep and vice versa. In the absence of goats, sheep will occupy typical goat territory, just as goats will occupy grasslands and other areas normally associated with sheep.

Early goats radiated out from western Asia. The markhor, a species that is similar to these early goats, still lives in that region. Other goats found advantages in colonizing some new territories. Generally speaking, the farther away from their ancestral home, the more likely these goats were to adopt sheeplike strategies if the need arose. The blue sheep, native of the Himalayas, is really a goat, although males have no beard or hairless areas on the carpal (ankle) joints. Males also lack the distinctive billy goat odor.

But while the observation of such species indicates a successful blurring of distinctions, it also points to a troubling problem. The wild goats and sheep have shown their survival skills in a series of increasingly remote ecological outposts, but ironically they have been forced there by their own kind.

DOMESTICATION

Goats and sheep have been domesticated and selectively bred for almost 10,000 years. They adapt to a range of agricultural conditions, particularly unproductive upland regions. Domestic goats are aggressive and agile, finding food and even thriving in areas where other domestic animals cannot survive. Lacking the sense of symbiosis with their surroundings displayed by their wild relatives, herds of domestic goats have eaten their way across great swaths of land in the Mediterranean and Middle East regions. The area known as Mesopotamia, between the Tigris and Euphrates Rivers, was once a fertile

Jean Paul Ferrero/Ardea

Ibex trophies in Italy testify to this resourceful species's status among sportsmen (above).

854

Bruce Coleman Ltd.

*This map shows the former and current ranges of
the American bighorn sheep.*

| FORMER RANGE | CURRENT RANGE |

**The American bighorn sheep were once
common throughout western North
America. At the high point of the last ice
age (about 18,000 years ago), they ranged
from Alaska down to Mexico. Incursions by
humans and imported Caprinae species
drove them off their more lowland (mainly
badland and desert) habitats. They are now
more or less secure, but restricted to a
number of separate mountain regions.**

basin that, over the last few millenia, supported the
Sumerians, Assyrians, Babylonians, and other great
civilizations. Mesopotamia is now a dust bowl, and its
demise resulted partly from the excessive grazing of
domestic animals, including sheep and goats. Erosion
and desertification are the more dramatic results of
goat damage, but less widely remarked are the ways
in which wild species suffer. For example, contact
with domestic varieties exposes wild goats and sheep
to a number of destructive parasites and diseases,
against which they have little or no resistance.

Wild sheep and goats are threatened in many
parts of the Himalayas, where uncontrolled hunting
adds to the destructive competition from domestic
species. The remote, almost inaccessible Himalayan
valleys are a refuge for many species, but they can

*Barbary sheep have been imported into the United
States, where their grazing is highly destructive.*

OUT OF ACTION

Wild goats and sheep lose out to their domestic counterparts in more ways than simply in competing for food supplies. Diseases and parasites, to which domestic species have built up defenses, can wipe out wild species. Hoof-and-mouth disease, contracted because of contact with domestic animals, can spread through saiga herds with frightening rapidity.

American bighorn sheep are particularly susceptible to such threats; moreover, they face an additional threat. Desert-dwelling Old World species have been introduced to the bighorn's native range. Unlike the bighorn, they are resistant to many of the diseases and parasites. The wild sheep in some parts of New Mexico and Arizona are now "exotic" species, such as the Persian wild goat and the Barbary sheep.

also become prisons with ever-dwindling food supplies if they are colonized by domestic species. This has occurred among isolated populations of markhors, urials, and argalis.

An extinct single-species genus, the cave goat, a historical footnote now, was an early victim of competition with domestic species. It lived in great numbers on the Balearic Islands off the Spanish coast. Faced with the invasion of humans and their domestic animals about 7,000 years ago, the cave goat gradually lost control of its island habitat and became extinct. The most recent remains date from around 3,800 years ago.

The position of chamois in Greece is a more recent example of the pressures that wild species face. The mountain meadows of the Hellenic ranges form traditional habitats for the chamois, but Greece also has a long tradition of rural pastoralism. Small farms with upland grazing are common throughout the country. Recent studies of chamois in Greece found populations drastically down from previous figures, with most evidence of chamois activity in protected areas such as national parks and game reserves. Significantly, the only sighting of chamois grazing in mountain meadows was at Mount Olympus, the most famous and highest mountain in the country.

Conservationists in developed countries are placed in a familiar—and awkward—position if they try to lecture disadvantaged farmers on more ecologically friendly methods of husbandry. Ownership of a domestic goat, the "poor man's cow," is often the only thing separating a farming family from starvation.

John Johnston/Oxford Scientific Films

ENDANGERED SPECIES

THE MOUFLON

The mouflon (MOOF-lon), or wild sheep of Europe, is a native of arid mountainous regions. It is the smallest of all the wild sheep; even the largest males rarely exceed 30 in (75 cm) in height and 120 lb (55 kg) in weight. The male's horns are long and spiraling, with the tips often pointing inward. The underfleece is extremely woolly, with a coarser, blackish brown winter covering featuring a distinctive white saddle patch. This patch is absent in females and young; males also lose it in the summer.

Mouflon are active around dawn and dusk. They never wander far, even when food is scarce, being able to eat nearly any available plants, including some that are poisonous to other mammals. The mouflon live in separate groups for much of the year, with rams staying clear of females and young. During the November rut, a mature ram detaches a female from the herd and mates with her. Fierce fights sometimes develop between males during the rut—particularly if an old ram is challenged—but serious injuries are rare.

Mouflon originated in the highlands of southwest Asia, adapting to sparse coverings of grass and herbs on the open ground at high altitude. There they were domesticated some 10,000 years ago; today's domestic sheep are descended mainly from mouflon. Habitat competition from domestic sheep, coupled with hunting, began to affect mouflon numbers in

CONSERVATION MEASURES

• The International Union for the Conservation of Nature (IUCN) classified the Nilgiri tahr as vulnerable after poaching and destruction of its habitat (the Nilgiri Hills of southern India) had reduced populations severely. Under this new protection, numbers have stabilized at around 2,200.

• Uncontrolled hunting and displacement by domestic livestock threatened both the West Caucasian and East Caucasian tur in the

their original range, although Marco Polo observed herds of hundreds during the 13th century.

Wildlife refuges in the former Soviet Union protect certain subspecies, such as the Nura-tau wild sheep and the roundhorn sheep, but mouflon as a whole are still threatened in Turkey, Afghanistan, Pakistan, and northern India. Mouflon seem most secure at the westernmost outposts of their range, on the islands of Corsica and Sardinia. Numbers there are still small—possibly as low as 700—but populations are stable enough to support exports to the European mainland. The overall "immigrant" population in Germany, Austria, Hungary, and the Czech Republic is now around 60,000.

CAPRINAE IN DANGER

THIS CHART SHOWS THOSE SPECIES LISTED BY THE INTERNATIONAL UNION FOR THE CONSERVATION OF NATURE (IUCN) IN THE *RED DATA BOOK*:

WEST CAUCASIAN TUR	RARE
EAST CAUCASIAN TUR	RARE
MARKHOR	ENDANGERED
NUBIAN IBEX	INDETERMINATE
WALIA IBEX	ENDANGERED
MAINLAND SEROW	INDETERMINATE
FORMOSAN SEROW	VULNERABLE
HIMALAYAN TAHR	INSUFFICIENTLY KNOWN
NILGIRI TAHR	VULNERABLE
ARABIAN TAHR	VULNERABLE
LONG-TAILED GORAL	INDETERMINATE

IN ADDITION, MORE THAN FORTY-FIVE RACES OR SUBSPECIES OF URIAL, MARKHOR, TAHR, MOUFLON, BIGHORN SHEEP, AND OTHER GOAT ANTELOPE ARE LISTED BY THE IUCN.

Mary Clay/Planet Earth Pictures

THE MAGNIFICENT MOUFLON, ANCESTOR OF THE DOMESTIC SHEEP, IS NOW DESPERATELY RARE.

beginning of this century. Regulated hunting and the establishment of preserves have helped populations in some areas, but attempts to establish these species outside their natural range have failed.

• The Israeli government protects the Nubian ibex, which is hunted mercilessly elsewhere in its natural range. Under this protection, these ibexes have become much less fearful of humans.

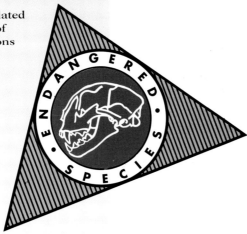

Trying to promote the cause of rare caprine at the expense of the farmer's livelihood is like trying to halt the harvesting of opium poppies or coca leaves elsewhere in the world.

THE SAIGA'S SALVATION

Human intervention, paradoxically, offers some unexpected lifelines to some threatened species. Saigas are a case in point. Last-minute conservation measures by the recently dissolved Soviet Union kept the species from extinction in the years immediately after World War I (see page 859). A series of severe winters in the late 1940s and early 1950s looked set to wipe out these gains. The winter of 1953–1954 alone killed 80,000 of the 180,000 reestablished saigas. But that is where the difference between natural and man-made disaster shows. Unlike the systematic exterminations of the 1700s and 1800s, the harsh winters of the 20th century prompted natural responses on the part of the saigas.

Conditioned by countless generations of evolution through occasionally severe winters, the surviving saigas did what came naturally—they literally ran for their lives. Rather than stay and freeze to death, healthy saigas dispersed to seek out less severe conditions. In these circumstances saigas can cover up to 30 miles (50km) a day. That is the final paradox of this story: The forced dispersal meant that the saigas reclaimed much of their lost territory.

FOR TROPHY AND TRADE

Many caprine species have been hunted for thousands of years, usually for their meat or because other parts of their bodies could be put to some use. The flesh of the chamois is tanned into the supple

857

leather called shammy, which is used to polish cars and clean glass. Musk ox horns have long been used by the Inuit people to make bows. During the 17th century, miraculous powers were ascribed to numerous parts of the ibex's body. Its blood was used as an antidote to poison and a cure for kidney stones; its dung was believed to be beneficial to sufferers of arthritis, tuberculosis, gout, and sciatica; and its horn, when ground up or boiled in milk, was used in gynecological applications. Demand became so great that an "ibex pharmacy" was established by the bishop of Salzburg, Austria.

These diverse reasons for hunting goat antelope led to the killing of thousands of individual animals. However, they were nothing like the craze for trophy hunting, which reached its peak in Europe and North America at the turn of the century and which still continues in many parts of the world.

> IBEX HAVE BEEN REINTRODUCED TO PARTS OF GERMANY, SPAIN, AND ON THE CARPATHIAN MOUNTAINS

High-powered hunting rifles, with long-distance sights, have disproved the idea of mountain ranges as inaccessible refuges.

The most sought-after trophies are the spectacular long-horned species such as the markhor and ibex. Mounted heads of markhor, with their unmistakable spiraling horns, are highly coveted. In the southern reaches of this species' range—across Afghanistan, northern Pakistan, and India—the markhor habitats have been reduced to a few isolated areas with small populations. The Nubian ibex is hunted heavily throughout its natural range near

ALONGSIDE MAN

THE POOR MAN'S COW

The domestication of sheep and goats is seen as one of the milestones in the social development of humans. Its importance is often compared with the discovery of fire. Asian wild sheep such as the mouflon were a vital source of meat for the hunting and gathering tribes who developed in southwest Asia. They were also the first animals to be domesticated, more than 9,000 years ago in the Middle East. Goats were first domesticated about 1,000 years later. Both sheep and goats provided meat, milk, and hides, with sheep taking on the still-important role as providers of wool.

Early sheep breeds resembled their ancestors such as the mouflon. Selective breeding was a successful way of introducing more wool or meat into the strain. The raising of sheep exclusively for wool developed in Spain during the 14th century. Their successful breeds, such as the merino, were exported, notably to Australia where they are at the top of the wool trade today.

There are well over a billion domestic sheep in the world today. The many breeds fall within one of two general classifications based on their coat type: hairy sheep, raised primarily for milk and meat; and wool sheep, whose fluffy fleeces are not shed seasonally. Domestic goats, numbering approximately 430 million worldwide, are raised for meat, milk, and goatskin.

Introduced into New Zealand in 1904, the Himalayan tahr is now so numerous that it has become a pest.

the Upper Nile Valley and in the Arabian Peninsula. Hunters set up blinds made of stones at water holes in the highlands. The ibex are seriously threatened if they venture into open ground lower down; they are usually met with a rain of bullets from bands of motorized hunters.

Several species of exotic ungulates, including Siberian and Persian ibex, have been introduced into the United States as game animals. The first four Siberian ibex were brought to Albuquerque, New Mexico, in 1962; since then these have been joined by many more. Exotic game ranching is now a massive commercial venture in Texas.

The American bighorn sheep is the most highly prized hunting trophy in North America, as it was for thousands of years to the Native Americans. Widespread recognition about conservation, coupled with the bighorn's remote habitat, have considerably reduced the numbers lost to hunters. But the bighorn faces other threats. Barbary sheep, imported as domestic animals to the American southwest around 1900, have escaped from farms and into the countryside. In many areas of the bighorn's natural range, these Barbary sheep have taken over as the dominant species, causing more harm to the bighorns than the cold-blooded hunters who preceded them. ∎

Peter Atkinson/Planet Earth Pictures

INTO THE FUTURE

The greatest security afforded to goat antelope is the remoteness of their habitats, but this alone cannot guarantee survival. Paradoxically, some of the rarest species, such as the goral, Arabian tahr, argali, and American bighorn sheep, live in areas that are far from large human populations. And ironically, it is in highly populated areas, such as western Europe, that effective measures have been taken to protect certain species.

The musk ox was saved from threatened extinction, and its numbers have risen under legislation. It withstood contact with local Inuits for millenia, but increased human activity in the Arctic during the 19th century escalated into a threat to its survival. Demand for musk ox skin led to the wholesale slaughter of the animals. During the 1880s alone the Hudson Bay Company sold more than 5,400 musk ox skins. Others were slaughtered to feed explorers

PREDICTION

DOMESTIC CONFLICT

Conservation laws will probably save high-profile species from hunting, but loss of habitat to domestic species and to humans will continue for many other species. The wild goat will probably disappear as it becomes increasingly hybridized with feral domestic goats.

and their sled dogs on the dozens of polar explorations. Even would-be conservation methods, such as shipping specimens away to zoos, backfired when it was revealed that five or six adult musk oxen died as a result of the capture of a single calf.

The Canadian government responded in 1917 by placing the musk ox under protection. Populations began to climb upward again, so that by the 1970s a limited cull was introduced on some Arctic islands. Similar measures, including the establishment of a national park, restored numbers in Greenland. There are now nearly 50,000 musk oxen in Canada and about half that number in Greenland.

The other way of restoring overall populations is to reestablish species in areas where they had once thrived. This has worked with the North American mountain goat. Hunting had caused many local populations to plummet by the middle of this century. Introduced herds of mountain goat, have thrived in Colorado, Montana, South Dakota, and selected areas on the northwest coast of North America. ■

THE SAIGA SAGA

Saigas once ranged across all of the Eurasian steppes and plains, but this range dwindled as saigas were hunted mercilessly in the early 1800s. The period after World War I saw populations down to only 1,000 or so, and extinction seemed imminent. In 1919, however, help came in the form of the fledgling Federation of Russian Soviet Republics, which issued a hunting ban on saiga. A similar ban was issued in 1923 by the Republic of Kazakhstan. Herd sizes soared in much of the western edge of the saiga's traditional range.

Since the breakup of the Soviet Union in 1991, there has been some uncertainty about the saiga's future. The newly independent states might now be tempted to turn a blind eye to large-scale hunting, seeing it as an earner of precious foreign currency.

IBEX SUCCESS

The Alpine ibex has long been a hunter's ultimate trophy, and its curative powers made it a valuable quarry. By the 1800s it faced extinction. In 1827, the remaining sixty or so ibex, which lived in the Gran Paradiso region of Italy, received protection. In the meantime, ibex were smuggled from Italy to two Swiss game parks, where breeding programs reestablished populations in Switzerland. Ibex did so well in both countries that foresters and farmers began to complain, and in 1977 strict cull measures were introduced. Ibex were released in other Alpine countries, and the total population now stands at about 22,000.

Illustration Carol Roberts

GORILLAS

RELATIONS

Gorillas are members of the great ape family, Pongidae. Other great apes include:

ORANGUTANS

CHIMPANZEES

PYGMY CHIMPANZEE

Adrian Warren/Ardea

CLASSIFICATION

The gorilla belongs to the great ape family, Pongidae, which also contains the chimp, pygmy chimp, and orangutan. The great apes are linked with the nine species of gibbons of the Hylobatidae family. Both ape families belong to the primate order, which also includes humans.

ORDER

Primates

FAMILY

Pongidae
(great apes)

GENUS

Gorilla

SPECIES

gorilla

SUBSPECIES

G. gorilla gorilla
(western lowland)

G. gorilla graueri
(eastern lowland)

G. gorilla beringei
(mountain)

KING OF THE APES

THE GORILLA DOES NOT HAVE THE FLUID AGILITY OF A GIBBON, NOR
CAN IT RIVAL THE CHIMP'S UNWITTING ABILITY TO PARODY MAN, BUT AS
A PRIMEVAL EXPRESSION OF POWER IT HAS NO EQUAL AMONG PRIMATES

Those fortunate enough to have seen gorillas in the wild recall the experience through many emotions: awe, wonder, delight—and naked fear. Delighted to find in the deepest jungle a species that could raise an eyebrow and stare in bemused curiosity at its distant cousin; awed at the bulk of a mature male—and terrified by his sudden charges. Whatever their reaction to this most regal of apes, few witnesses are likely ever to forget an encounter.

The gorilla is one of thirteen species of apes. The nine species of lesser apes are all gibbons of the family Hylobatidae, which are found in India, China, and Southeast Asia. The great apes, family Pongidae, are the gorilla, chimpanzee, pygmy chimpanzee, and orangutan. The first three of these are African, while the orang lives in the jungles of Borneo and Sumatra. Apes are quite distinct from monkeys, although both groups belong to the important and extremely diverse primate order.

The ancestry of the primates is a subject of much debate and probably always will be, since it involves the origins of *Homo sapiens*. The fossil record is said to begin with a tooth from Montana, dated at about seventy million years old, that probably belonged to a primate. The very earliest primates were small and squirrel-like, with mobile limbs and articulate fingers. They probably ate insects, later developing a taste for the abundant fruit to be found in the permanently moist tropical forests.

The Old World primates can be traced back some 40 million years to *Parapithecus* (pah-rah-PITH-ek-uss), a small monkey with an apelike skull. About 20–30 million years ago, the apes and ancestral humans split from the Old World monkeys. An early ancestor of apes and humans was *Proconsul africanus* (pro-KON-sul aff-ri-KAHN-us). Roughly the size of a baboon, *Proconsul* leaped or ran about in the forests of East Africa, feeding on fruit.

Ken Lucas

The gorilla is the least arboreal of the apes, due in part to the adult male's phenomenal bulk (above).

Len Rue Jr. /Bruce Coleman Ltd.

BIG HEAD

Mature males are instantly recognizable by the prominent crest on the head. This is a mass of tissue and muscle built up around a bony ridge called a sagittal crest. The crest provides an anchorage for the long temporal muscles; these stretch down the cheeks and operate the lower jaw. But why does the female not also have such a huge head?

All gorillas eat vegetation, and as such they need big muscles to power their cheek teeth. But a fully mature male (called a silverback, is the backbone of a social group; as its defense and its stud male, he is far larger than any other gorilla in the group. And to fuel his huge bulk, he needs plenty of food—all of which needs to be chewed thoroughly and requires the extensive musculature found on the enlarged cranium. In addition, the big head helps to avoid bloodshed; it expresses a dominant silverback's size and power before any potential rivals get ideas about taking him on in a fight.

By about fifteen million years ago, several ape forms had evolved, both large and small. What the large apes gained in brute strength they lost in agility. Unable to scamper upon branches like monkeys, they swung along by their arms from tree to tree, many evolving short legs and long arms to suit this mode of travel. They also lost the tail, which was no longer needed for balance.

Apes dispersed widely when Africa drifted into Asia. These Asian apes, which would ultimately give rise to the gibbons and orangutans, diverged from the African apes some 12.5 million years ago. At some point between eight and four million years ago, early man, the chimp, and the gorilla began to evolve along three independent paths.

GORILLAS TODAY

Today there is one species of gorilla, represented by three races living in equatorial Africa. Smallest is the western lowland gorilla, *Gorilla gorilla gorilla*, which inhabits low-lying rain forests from extreme southeastern Nigeria into southern Congo. More than 600 miles (1,000 km) away to the east can be found the eastern lowland gorilla, *G. g. graueri*. It is the largest race, confined to pockets of rain forest in eastern Zaire. Not far away, among the Virunga

Proud as a prize bull, a silverback shows off the profile of his impressive physique.

volcanoes of Zaire, Rwanda, and Uganda, lives probably the most famous of them all: the mountain gorilla, *G. g. beringei*. Unknown to western scientists before the 19th century, this great ape is now notoriously rare, with only 400–650 surviving in the wild.

The three races have their own distinguishing characteristics. The western lowland gorilla has small jaws and teeth set in a broad face. The eastern lowland race has short, black body hair and a narrow face, but is probably the largest of the three. The mountain gorilla is the hairiest of them all, owing to its cool, moist, high-altitude home, and also has a very broad face armed with massive jaws and teeth. All in all there are probably thirty identifiable distinctions between lowland and mountain gorillas.

These differences are, however, relatively subtle, so the three races probably diverged fairly recently. The mountain gorilla, in particular, is genetically very close to the eastern lowland race. One theory is that gorillas originated in the lowland forests of Cameroon, West Africa, then migrated east as far as the Rift Valley. In this way they would have occupied a continuous band of moist tropical forest from west to east. It is thought that a dry period occurring about a million years ago eradicated the intervening forests in what is now Zaire, separating the western gorillas from their eastern brethren. In any case, the volcanic habitat of the mountain gorilla only erupted into existence between 500,000 and 20,000 years ago, and in the grand scheme of primate evolution, this is but a brief moment in time. ∎

BLOOD BROTHERS

Today, most experts believe that humans and apes diverged less than eight million years ago. Many world religions refute the existence of any ancestral link whatsoever, preferring explanations that involve divine creation. However, modern genetic research seems to favor the former theory.

In looks alone, we bear resemblance to the apes beyond superficial differences of skeletal, muscle, and facial structure. And on a biochemical level, we are very similar to them indeed: In our blood serums and chromosomes we are closer than the orangutans to the African apes. Scientists use the term *genome* to sum up the total genetic information passed on to an offspring by its parent. Our genome differs from those of the gorilla and chimp by less than 2 percent. Genetically speaking, we are more closely related to the apes than, say, zebras are to horses.

B/W illustrations Ruth Grewcock and Peter David Scott

WESTERN LOWLAND GORILLA

G. gorilla gorilla

(G. goh-RILL-ah goh-RILL-ah)

The first gorilla to be known to western science, this shy ape lives in the tropical jungles of the Congo Basin. The adult male has a distinctive near-white saddle. Its social units are smaller than those of the mountain gorilla, and it moves around more during the day. Relatively little is known in detail about its habits. Total population is estimated at about 40,000.

EASTERN LOWLAND GORILLA

G. gorilla graueri

(goh-RILL-ah GRA-wer-ee)

Living in the moist Zaire rain forests, close to the Uganda-Rwanda borders in the western Rift Valley, this subspecies is probably the largest of the three. It has characteristically short, black fur. Members of this race are occasionally mistaken for mountain gorillas, which live nearby. There are probably 4,000–10,000 surviving today in Zaire.

ORANGUTANS   GIBBONS

The apes comprise the gibbons, family Hylobatidae, and the great apes, family Pongidae. In the past some scientists wanted to classify all the African apes—the two chimps and the gorilla—in the genus Pan, *to reinforce the fact that they are more closely related to each other than to the orangutan of Asia.*

MOUNTAIN GORILLA

G. gorilla berengei
(*goh-RILL-ah BEH-ren-gay*)

Hairiest of the three subspecies, the mountain gorilla is certainly the most famous. It has been very much in the public eye ever since Dian Fossey spent two decades studying it in its montane habitat of the Virunga volcano region in Rwanda, Uganda, and Zaire. Its black hair grows long and silky as an adaptation to its cold, misty, high-altitude environment. Penned in on all sides by a soaring human population, the mountain gorilla and its habitat are under intense pressure.

Color illustrations Steve Kingston

HUMANS

CHIMPS

APES

PROSIMIANS

NEW WORLD
MONKEYS

OLD WORLD
MONKEYS

ALL PRIMATES

865

ANATOMY:
THE GORILLA

The gorilla often stands shorter than a tall adult man, let down mainly by its bandy-legged stance. The tallest gorilla subspecies is the eastern lowland (above left), which may reach 5.9 ft (180 cm) in height. The female (above right) can reach about 4.9 ft (150 cm). In weight and build, however, gorillas beat humans every time.

THE EYES

are small and deep-set beneath the prominent brow, and are a warm midbrown in color. They give good vision and can communicate the ape's moods and emotions very expressively.

THE NOSTRILS

are broad and flattened. The surrounding nasal wings are wrinkled and shaped in a highly personalized manner on each individual. The sense of smell is good; a gorilla can, for example, detect a human's presence at 65 ft (20 m) or more.

SILVERBACK KNUCKLE PRINT

SILVERBACK FOOTPRINT

JUVENILE KNUCKLE PRINT

FEMALE FOOTPRINT

TRACK IMPRINTS

Although the gorilla can easily walk upright like us, it prefers to amble on all fours, resting the weight of the forequarters on its knuckles. The impressions show up well on a muddy forest floor. The footprints look similar to ours, except that the gorilla's opposable big toe is visibly set apart from the rest of the foot.

SKELETON

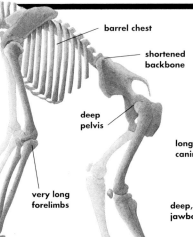

The skeleton reflects a lifestyle more typical of the gibbon or even the orang. These are the experts at swinging through trees by their long arms, while an adult gorilla is more or less confined to the ground. As hangers and swingers, apes also need fewer lumbar vertebrae (the bones in the lower back), having only four or so compared with the six or seven in a monkey.

barrel chest

shortened backbone

deep pelvis

very long forelimbs

SILVERBACK SKULL

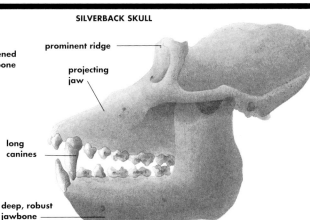

prominent ridge

projecting jaw

long canines

deep, robust jawbone

THE BODY

is huge and muscular, particularly in the male. The prominent rump and forequarters give the gorilla a slim-waisted profile when on all fours, but the torso slumps heavily when the animal sits down.

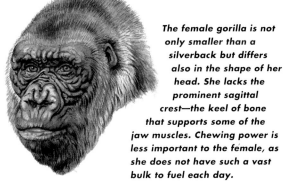

The female gorilla is not only smaller than a silverback but differs also in the shape of her head. She lacks the prominent sagittal crest—the keel of bone that supports some of the jaw muscles. Chewing power is less important to the female, as she does not have such a vast bulk to fuel each day.

ADULT FEMALE GORILLA

THE HAIR

grows longest and silkiest on the mountain subspecies—especially on the long forearms—to cope with the inclement weather conditions. An adult male is known as a silverback because the hair over his lumbar region turns a silver-gray.

THE HANDS

are huge, with thick fingers. The knuckles grow calloused with age, because the ape rests on them when on all fours. The thumbs are opposable, and each digit has a flattened nail.

THE FEET

support the gorilla's weight from heel to toe. They are less handlike than those of the chimp, although the big toe, like the thumb, is capable of grasping.

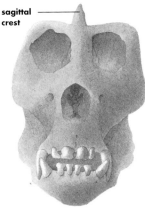

FACT FILE:

MOUNTAIN GORILLA

CLASSIFICATION

GENUS: *GORILLA*

SPECIES: *GORILLA BERINGEI*

SIZE

STANDING HEIGHT/MALE: 4–5.7 FT (125–175 CM)

STANDING HEIGHT/FEMALE: AROUND 5 FT (150 CM)

ARM SPAN: 6.6–9 FT (2–2.75 M)

CHEST SPAN: UP TO 20 IN (50 CM)

WEIGHT/MALE: 365 LB (165 KG) ON AVERAGE

WEIGHT/FEMALE: 185 LB (85 KG) ON AVERAGE

WEIGHT AT BIRTH: 4.4 LB (2 KG)

COLORATION

THE MOUNTAIN GORILLA HAS LONG, SILKY BLACK HAIR OVER MOST OF THE BODY, WHILE THE EASTERN LOWLAND GORILLA HAS SHORTER HAIR OF SIMILAR COLOR. IN BOTH THESE SUBSPECIES THE SILVERBACK'S SADDLE IS RESTRICTED TO THE BACK THE WESTERN LOWLAND GORILLA HAS A BROWNISH-GRAY COAT; THE SILVERBACK'S SADDLE EXTENDS TO THE THIGHS AND RUMP

FEATURES

ADULT MALE IS MASSIVE, WITH MUSCULAR LIMBS AND A THICKSET, POT-BELLIED TORSO, AS WELL AS A HIGH-DOMED HEAD AND A SILVER-GRAY SADDLE BOTH SEXES ARE LARGER THAN THE CHIMPANZEE, WHICH OTHERWISE LOOKS SIMILAR TO THE GORILLA JUVENILE MALES LACK THE SILVER BACK NEWBORN GORILLAS LOOK ALMOST HUMAN

SILVERBACK SKULL

sagittal crest

SKULL

The gorilla's jaw projects less dramatically from the cranial mass than that of the chimpanzee. Nevertheless the jaw is deep and strong, providing extensive anchorage for operative muscles. In the silverback (left), these muscles are supported also by the sagittal crest—a long bony ridge similar to the keel of a boat. This crest grows as the male matures. The skull is clearly similar to that of humans, with the large braincase and forward-facing eyes typical of apes and hominids.

forward-facing eyes

large braincase

FEMALE GORILLA SKULL

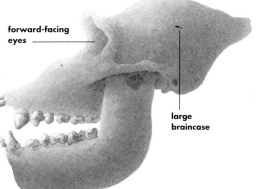

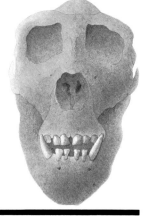

BENEVOLENT GIANTS

GORILLA GROUPS ARE LARGELY ORGANIZED AROUND A SINGLE SILVERBACK. THE FEMALES USUALLY FOLLOW HIS LEAD BUT WILL FORM COALITIONS TO COUNTERACT UNPOPULAR MOVES

G orillas live in a close-knit group or troupe, which is led by a single dominant male. They forage each day through the lush forest undergrowth, ambling on their feet and knuckles and occasionally climbing into the trees. They rise with the sun, and, when it sets, settle down to sleep in a leafy nest. Gorillas luxuriate in restful inactivity, dozing perhaps thirteen hours each night and then spending some two-fifths of their waking hours resting quietly or sunbathing. The remaining daylight hours are passed mostly in feeding and traveling.

A DAY IN THE LIFE

Within an hour or so of sunrise, a gorilla group rouses itself with a bout of yawning and scratching. When the silverback awakes, the rest draw close to him in anticipation—for he usually leads their daily routine. It is time for breakfast. Finding the nearest patch of lush saplings and shrubs, the gorillas settle down to feed for two or three hours. Since each finds its own personal patch of food, the group is typically spread over about 2,700 sq ft (250 sq m) of semiopen forest, but they stay in touch with occasional hoots.

By midmorning the group has eaten its fill and is ready for a nap. Gathering again around the silverback, the apes settle down for a long siesta. If the day is fine, most of them sprawl supine, or slump against the nearest tree trunk, to soak up the sun.

If it rains during the nap, the apes may well not bother to seek shelter but instead simply squat down and tuck their head between their drawn-up knees. Gorillas have been seen to huddle for hours in the rain, seemingly in utter misery but too apathetic to find shelter. Typically unpredictable, the same groups have been seen on other days to leap as one for the nearest tree during a downpour. They crowd around the trunk, a squabbling, heaving mass of sodden apes pushing one another into the wet.

During a fine day's siesta, juvenile males—those under nine years old, still with a black back—may wander about, making awkward passes at females; these approaches are usually rebuffed. The infants truly exploit this period, since they are not trying to keep up with adults on the move through the forest. They fiddle with bits of greenery, wrestle gamely, clamber up and then slide down liana vines, and even play king of the castle on anthills. A mother will use this quiet time to groom her infant, putting it over a knee or arm and combing through the hairs. She is especially careful to keep the anus clean. Just like a human, the infant gorilla objects to her attentions but cannot escape her firm grip. The siesta may run on well into the midafternoon—by which time bellies are once again empty, so the group forages again. As before, they spread out to feed.

A NEST FOR THE NIGHT

At some point in the early evening the silverback builds his nest, and the others follow his lead. Since gorillas spend the day wandering in search of fresh browse, they build a new nest each evening. Each gorilla stands in a patch of shrub and breaks low saplings or runners toward itself, trampling them down. Standing up, it treads low, springy herbs with one foot, then presses down the brushy stems with both palms. Within five minutes, it has constructed a naturally springy, bowl-shaped bed that neatly cups and supports its bulky body.

Gorillas sometimes build nests up in the trees. In the Impenetrable Forest of Uganda, for example, they nest up in the bamboo canopy or in low trees at least as often as upon the forest floor. In other areas, they stay low. Owing to their mountainous bulk, adult males very rarely leave the ground. ∎

On the rainy, misty Virunga volcanoes, long fur is a distinct advantage to the mountain gorilla.

Art Wolfe/Tony Stone Worldwide

John Cancalosi/Bruce Coleman Ltd.

ANGRY OUTBURSTS

Gorillas are not always gentle; silverbacks in particular give rein to their emotions with apparently terrifying displays.

Chest beating usually follows a ritualized pattern. The male first utters a series of hoots, which slowly swell to a throbbing cacophony. After a minute or so of hooting, the male rears up on his feet, rips up some vegetation, and hurls it into the air. Then, cupping his hands, he drums on his lower chest for a couple of seconds, sending out a loud "pok-pok-pok." Kicking a limb into the air, he then leaps sideways and slams his palms violently upon the ground. These last few acts last only about five seconds in all.

There are many variations on the theme. Sometimes a gorilla beats not upon its chest but upon its head or thighs, or even upon another gorilla's back. At other times it performs single-handed while hanging from a tree bough.

Among its many call sounds, the gorilla may use an ear-shattering "scream-roar" in anger or as a warning to the group.

HABITATS

All three subspecies of gorillas live in the wet tropical forests of Africa. Within this environment, however, they exploit different habitat types. The mountain gorillas are restricted to semiopen forests on cool uplands, while the lowland gorillas, especially the western subspecies, have access to more dense forests.

LUSH LOWLANDS

The western lowland gorilla far outnumbers the eastern and mountain races and is correspondingly more widespread. It is, however, less well known in its habits. It has received a minimum of attention, at least when compared to the much-publicized events surrounding the work of Dian Fossey and other researchers among the mountain apes. The western race lives in the Central African Republic, equatorial Guinea, Gabon, and western Congo at least as far east as the Congo River. It also occurs in tiny, isolated areas of northwestern Cameroon.

This lowland distributional range constitutes a significant percentage of the Congo Basin—a vast area within which some four-fifths of Africa's tropical rain forests can be found. The moist jungles drain away into the mighty Ubangi and Congo Rivers, which reach the Atlantic coast at the northwestern

King of the hill: During mealtimes, the silverback often has first refusal of the choicest feeding spot.

Daniel J. Cox/Oxford Scientific Films

KEY FACTS

● The Parc des Volcans, which includes the southeastern sector of the Virungas, occupies only 0.5 percent of Rwanda's land area yet traps 10 percent of the country's total annual rainfall.

● In the Afro-alpine zone of the Virunga summits, giant plants abound. These include huge varieties of *Senecio*, which are tiny weeds in more temperate climates but reach heights of 20 ft (6 m) or more up on the volcanoes. They flower only once every ten to twenty years in the cold, wet climate.

● Mountain gorillas dislike crossing any watercourse larger than a stream. When forced to do so, they will either use any existing stepping-stones or even push tree ferns over to make a crude bridge. Lowland gorillas have no objection to water.

● The extinct crater of Mt. Visoke is now a lake, replete with alpine vegetation. The two newest volcanoes, Mt. Nyiragongo and Mt. Nyamuragira, are still intermittently active.

corner of Angola. Even today, access to the remotest parts of the Congo Basin is primarily up the rivers by boat, and the waterside vegetation is especially dense and primed with thorns. Here, too, lives the tsetse fly, a vector of lethal sleeping sickness. It comes as no great surprise, therefore, that humans had until fairly recently made few inroads on the western lowland gorilla's domain. The western lowland gorilla stays at altitudes no higher than about 6,000 ft (1,800 m), so its homeland is never too cold.

MOUNTAIN LIVING

Far away to the east, in and around the Great Rift Valley, can be found the other two subspecies. The Rift Valley is a series of ranges and depressions brought about by geological forces over the last 200 million years. There are two rifts—eastern and western. The former cuts through Ethiopia and Kenya and curls to a halt around Tanzania to the east of Lake Victoria. The western rift starts in the northwest of Lake Victoria on the Zaire-Uganda border, continuing south along Lakes Albert, Edward, Kivu,

Tanganyika, and Malawi (Nyasa) into Mozambique. Toward the northern end of this western rift, the Virunga volcanoes are strung across the valley to the north of Lake Kivu, forming a natural three-way border between Zaire, Rwanda, and Uganda.

Before the genesis of the Virungas, Lake Kivu drained northward via a river on the western Rift Valley floor. Then, maybe half a million years ago, the volcanoes started to erupt. The last two to emerge did so only 20,000 years ago. As the succession of craters spewed lava across the valley floor, they built up a huge dam some 1,800 ft (550 m) thick and 15 miles (24 km) wide. Prevented from draining, Lake Kivu's water level slowly crept about 400 ft (120 m) up the walls of the Virungas until finally, some 4,000 years later, it could drain south into Lake Tanganyika via the Ruzizi River.

The mountain gorilla is found today in two small islands of suitable habitat in the Rift Valley. These are the Virunga volcanoes themselves and the nearby Impenetrable Forest of Uganda. There are claimed sightings of mountain gorillas on the upper slopes of Zaire's Kahuzi-Biega National Park, northwest of Lake Kivu, but these are more likely to be eastern lowland gorillas.

The mountain gorilla's range has much to do with its diet. It has evolved to feed mainly on leaves—perhaps to avoid competition with its fruit-eating

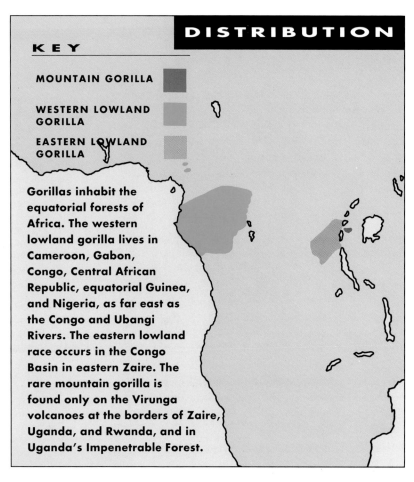

DISTRIBUTION

KEY

MOUNTAIN GORILLA

WESTERN LOWLAND GORILLA

EASTERN LOWLAND GORILLA

Gorillas inhabit the equatorial forests of Africa. The western lowland gorilla lives in Cameroon, Gabon, Congo, Central African Republic, equatorial Guinea, and Nigeria, as far east as the Congo and Ubangi Rivers. The eastern lowland race occurs in the Congo Basin in eastern Zaire. The rare mountain gorilla is found only on the Virunga volcanoes at the borders of Zaire, Uganda, and Rwanda, and in Uganda's Impenetrable Forest.

Adrian Warren/Ardea

neighbor the chimp, or perhaps simply because the ecological niche presented itself. Whatever the origin of this diet, such food is scarce on the dimly lit floor of the densest primary rain forests—too scarce, at any rate, for a hungry group of heavy apes. The gibbons, by contrast, can manage very well in the lush evergreen rain forests of Asia, because they possess a winning blend of a compact, lightweight body and powerful forearms. These aerial acrobats swing hand over hand through the high canopy in search of ripe fruit, selecting fresh food trees at will. Not so the gorilla; although adventurous youngsters often take to the branches, such activity is unwise for a quarter-ton silverback. Therefore, gorillas stick to the habitat that offers the most abundant, easy-to-grasp supplies of food; in eastern Africa, this means secondary forest.

Secondary forest is that which has been partially cleared and has regenerated—unlike primary forest, which is wholly untouched, least of all by man. In some forests gorillas actually benefit by the consequences of human activity; where, perhaps, farmers once made a few clearings for crops or cattle but have long since left the area. In the absence of tall,

Gorillas thrive best in forests where sunlight can penetrate clearings to encourage ground cover.

871

shady old trees, sunlight reaches through and the undergrowth stakes its claim on the fertile soil, eventually becoming a supermarket of green fodder for the slow-moving leaf-eaters. In the eastern African mountains, fresh plant growth is generated through not only human inroads but also natural causes, such as volcanic activity, elephant damage, rockfalls, and the cyclical die-offs of the local vegetation, in particular the midslope bamboo forests. Coupled with all these agents is the pervading moisture on the high Virunga slopes.

EASTERN LOWLANDS

Ten times rarer than its western cousin, the eastern lowland gorilla occurs across a correspondingly smaller range. It lives in patches of lowland rain forest and in the western foothills of the Rift Valley, all within eastern Zaire. On Mount Kahuzi, it keeps to altitudes of around 6,560–8,200 ft (2,000–2,500 m), whereas mountain gorillas in the Virunga range live at altitudes of 9,200–11,150 ft (2,800–3,400 m).

If we were to track a gorilla group through the forest, there would be key signs to look for. Gorillas bulldoze, like elephants; they lumber ponderously through the undergrowth often in single file, leaving a trail of broken stems. Fronds and sprays of foliage are ripped or frayed where a huge hand has swiped

Steve Turner/Oxford Scientific Films

FOCUS ON

THE VIRUNGA VOLCANOES

Rising to an altitude of 14,787 ft (4,507 m), the eight volcanoes of the Virunga range cannot quite match the 16,732 ft (5,100 m) of the Ruwenzori peaks to their north, but they have their own dramatic beauty. Like other African mountain ranges, they are an island haven for specialized, often unique plants and animals.

The lower slopes are clad in evergreen rain forest, where warthogs and bushbuck browse the vegetation. From an altitude of about 7,550 ft (2,300 m), bamboo thickets start to appear—these can grow to heights of 60 ft (18 m). Above the mixed bamboo and evergreen grow ancient forests of *Hagenia* trees. Around 50–60 ft (15–18 m) tall, the knotty boughs of this stocky species are draped in thick mosses and trailing lichens. Higher still lies a more open terrain scattered with huge heaths and lobelias. The bamboo and *Hagenia* forests are home to the mountain gorilla. On these subalpine slopes the atmosphere is thin, wet, and often freezing, but the ape has long, silky hair to fight the damp chill.

The entire Virunga range is now protected within national parks. Rwanda contains the Parc National des Volcans; Zaire holds the Parc National des Virunga; Uganda contributes the Kigezi Gorilla Sanctuary.

TEMPERATURE AND RAINFALL

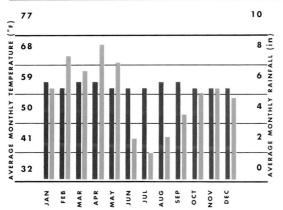

■ TEMPERATURE

■ RAINFALL

Near the equator, lowlands remain warm throughout the year, but up on the high Virunga slopes it is often very cold and wet. Mean annual rainfall is 72 in (183 cm). There may be more than two hours of rain daily from October to December.

at a snack. There are circular nests on the ground or up in the trees—but these may not necessarily be recent, since such nests remain distinguishable for up to a year. A clear indication that gorillas have just passed by would be their smell—pungent, like human sweat. It is particularly noticeable when a male has been frightened, as glands in his armpits release the rank perspiration in an automatic fear reaction. Other key signs are the copious heaps of dung, with their distinctive three-lobed stools, littered at random along the way. ■

NEIGHBORS

The mammals of the Virungas include those that can live only in the forests and those that thrive also in open country. Some species have adapted biologically to suit the high-altitude climate.

BONGO

This forest antelope skulks among the bamboo, relying on its patterned coat to conceal it from view.

BUSHPIG

Bushpigs roam energetically through the forests in small bands, browsing on plants and foraging in the topsoil.

Neighbor illustrations Craig Robson/Wildlife Art Agency

UGANDA

ZAIRE

RWANDA

Lake
Kivu

RED COLOBUS MONKEY

Up in the Virunga forests the red colobus grows an extra-woolly coat to cope with the cold conditions.

GOLDEN CAT

This cat preys on small mammals and birds in the forests and scrubland of West and central Africa.

CONGO PEAFOWL

This secretive cousin of the more familiar ornamental peacock was not known to science until 1936.

HAMMERHEADED BAT

Males gather at a lek to compete for mates. Their big heads naturally amplify their staccato mating calls.

CROWNED HAWK EAGLE

This supreme hunter can snatch monkeys from the forest canopy or swoop down upon duiker fawns.

FOOD AND FEEDING

Wild gorillas eat leaves, shoots, roots, bark, ripe fruits, and other plant parts. This offers so much diversity that they eat very little else; dozens of plant species may be included in their diet, and some lowland groups have been found to eat 95 different species of fruit. The amount of fruit eaten differs according to the region; among lowland gorillas it may comprise 50 percent of the diet, while on the Virungas it is barely significant. This variability has a profound effect on localized gorilla societies.

Gorillas prefer ripe fruit, and although there is more available fruit in a warm lowland forest in Congo, for example, than in the cold Virungas, there is still not a huge amount. Therefore, even a

---

GORILLAS WILL EAT SOIL, INSECTS, OR
EVEN THEIR OWN DUNG TO OBTAIN
POTASSIUM, CALCIUM, AND VITAMINS IN
AREAS OF LOW-GRADE VEGETATION

---

lowland gorilla group needs to make an effort to find the fruit. And since there is too little in any one spot to feed several hungry gorillas, these lowland groups tend to be smaller—about half the size, in fact, of those in eastern Africa. Interestingly, lowland gorillas have a correspondingly more muscular build than their upland relatives, as they spend more time and energy on foraging.

SUPPLY AND DEMAND

In the right place and time, a gorilla group might find itself up to the ears in forage—but gorillas are careful not to exhaust their food supplies. They take only so much from a small area, allowing the greenery to grow back. This food supply management is affected, too, by the regular tramplings of elephant and buffalo as they wind through the undergrowth. One of their favorite foods in equatorial Guinea is wild ginger—roots, fruits, seeds, and all. It is believed that the seeds will not germinate unless they have been ingested and passed through an animal gut.

Depending on where they live, gorillas rely heavily on certain foods. In Kabara, between Mt. Mikeno and Mt. Karisimbi, mountain gorillas eat about 30 different plants. They feast on wild celery, bedstraw, nettles, and thistles, and nibble on the fresh shoots of bamboo when available. For no clear reason they also chew the bark off certain trees, and they particularly like to strip plants, such as the celery, down to the tasty pith. Lowland

gorillas readily climb several feet up into trees to get to mistletoe and other favorites, then adopt any position necessary—even hanging precariously from their feet—in order to reach the food.

DINING SKILLS

Gorilla feeding methods are partly learned through experience. Infants watch their mothers feeding, sometimes even snatching a half-eaten morsel from the adult hand. They also taste foods that are clearly not on the standard menu, such as lichens: One taste of something nasty and the youngster quickly spits it out, whereupon the mother calmly removes the sample from her offspring's clutches. Bedstraw is a spiny local vine that needs a

FOLIAGE FEEDERS

Mountain gorillas feed mainly on foliage. There is so much of it in their habitat that they can usually sit back and gather it by the fistful (right).

Illustration Guy Troughton/Wildlife Art Agency

M. Harvey/Natural Science Photos

A gorilla's nimble hands are highly skilled at stripping out only the edible parts of plants.

special eating method. Adults pluck the stems carefully, then wind them into a tight, leafy wad on which they chew. Until the youngsters have learned to do this, they simply stuff the stems into their mouths like a child eating spaghetti. Sometimes, however, a young ape may display great dexterity as it runs a closed fist up a spray, stripping the leaves into a bite-sized rosette. Whatever gorillas eat, they pass it to the mouth with their hands.

All this eating means a great deal of dung. Where gorillas eat leafy food, the dung is crumbling and loose. Since they excrete wherever they are, including in the sleeping nest, the apes often roll in their dung. This matters little, since the fibrous dung does not stick, but any bamboo shoot or ripe fruit in the diet produces more liquefied droppings. ■

JUICY FRUIT

Lowland gorillas have access to fruit all year round in the forests of the Congo Basin.

*in*SIGHT

EASY NEIGHBORS

Because vegetation is abundant in their habitat, gorillas need not defend their food supplies. Therefore, different gorilla groups frequently overlap in range. When two groups meet, they are more likely to ignore each other than fight. Up to six different groups have been known to use the same patch of forest.

Nevertheless, gorillas do not simply wander anywhere. In some areas their travels are limited by poor habitat, such as open savanna or farmland; elsewhere their home range seems bound by invisible lines. Perhaps they become familiar from an early age with a particular area, and are reluctant to cross its subtly delineated boundaries into uncharted terrain.

SOCIAL STRUCTURE

With the exception of a few lone males, most gorillas live within a group led by a single silverback. There are usually between two and twenty individuals in a group, although there may be as many as 40. Groups tend to be smaller in denser lowland forest, or where food sources are more fruit-based and therefore scarcer. A typical small group includes a silverback plus a younger male, three adult females, and a couple of young. The assembly is in effect a harem, in which adult females have different ranks among themselves. Larger groups may contain three or four silverbacks, usually close relatives, plus several more females and subadult males, but each has his own ranking. There will still be one dominant silverback.

Few gorillas will dare to challenge the silverback,

THE SILVERBACK IS CENTRAL, WHILE
FEMALES DOMINATE JUVENILES AND
JUVENILES PULL RANK ACCORDING TO AGE

unless they are themselves a rival adult male; his sheer size inhibits any such insubordination. Unless the silverback senses a direct threat, he is unlikely to invest in aggressive confrontation. He takes care of the group, always facing up to deadly intruders such as human hunters or big leopards, and tolerates the infants that scramble over his vast potbelly during siesta time.

FEMALE TROUBLE
Adult females often have closest associations with their immature offspring, although adult females will often form bonds with each other. However, on those occasions when female compatibility is poor, the silverback will usually intervene when outright fighting occurs. Conversely, the females work cooperatively to keep silverback aggression in check when necessary. Altogether, gorilla groups remain relatively peaceable. In part, peace reigns because gorillas emigrate when the social circumstances are not working. Low-ranking females without peer support usually leave, as do untolerated, maturing juvenile males.

Young females are normally not attracted to males they have known since birth—usually their fathers and brothers—and normally seek new groups to join. Sexually mature at around

seven or eight years of age, females are first likely to breed at around ten years old. A female will normally join another, smaller group or even a lone male before doing so. She is a desirable asset to any aspiring silverback and will be warmly welcomed.

ROGUE MALES
Life is not easy for the young males, either. Since they are rarely allowed the favors of the harem, they must seek a mate elsewhere. So somewhere around the age of eleven a male's thoughts may turn to independence, although many young males stay in their natal group for life. When leaving, he loiters on the edge of the group for several months before finally separating. Many lonely years may follow for him, as he puts on the pounds and slowly turns silvery, building up his physical and social strength and all the while trying to lure away young females. This can lead him into trouble, as it may involve direct confrontation with a dominant silverback.

WIFE AND CHILD
The silverback begets as many youngsters as possible, and is highly protective toward his own mates and offspring. Females with the young of another male are likely to be tolerated (below).

PULLING RANK
The silverback often tolerates young males in his group, even tolerating some copulation with the females. Generally, this tolerance is extended only to sons and brothers (below).

Andrew Plumptre/Oxford Scientific Films

Conflict between females is usually resolved by eventual tolerance or emigration of the lower ranking female.

On such occasions, the rivals chest-beat vigorously, or pose erect on all fours and strut stiffly past each other, with elbows turned out to exaggerate the physique. This almost always results in a peaceful solution, with the young challenger usually backing down. Although lone males can be driven to desperate acts by the desire for a mate, actual fights are very rare. Gorillas often seem aggressive to people— usually because they have been taken by surprise in the forest—but they adopt more of a live-and-let-live policy with their own kind.

If a lone male manages to secure a mate, he is at least on the way toward acquiring a harem, and therefore a group, of his own—but such a goal is rarely achieved before he has turned fifteen. Once he reaches the exalted position of chief silverback he may control the group for several years. ∎

in SIGHT

COPING WITH DEATH

A young gorilla has only a 55 percent chance of surviving into its seventh year. Hunting, poaching, disease, and infanticide strike down about 20–25 percent of infants in their first year alone.

Mothers react in different ways to the loss of an offspring. In one instance, a formerly doting female became utterly detached from her infant when it died. Although she would not abandon the tiny corpse, she dragged it along as she walked, or simply crouched beside it as she stared into space. Finally, after a few days she left the crumpled body on the forest floor and moved on. This refusal to part with the deceased is apparently common among gorillas; when a member of the group dies, the others stand around and stare, as if uncertain whether the victim is truly dead.

Curiously, females have also been seen to prance childishly about after losing a child; perhaps they are relieved at the sense of freedom, or they are simply trying to throw off the sense of loss. Old females who lose a mate of long standing tend to become moody, while juveniles appear depressed after losing a mother. Luckily, an adult member of the group—even the silverback himself—usually takes the youngster into its protective care.

Illustration Lee Gibbons/Wildlife Art Agency

LIFE CYCLE

There are no clearly defined seasons in the warm, humid equatorial forests, and gorillas may breed in any month of the year. Mating will be more or less restricted to the dominant silverback, depending on his age, tolerance level, and powers of vigilance.

The females in the group breed every three to four years or so. They come into estrus for one to three days in every 27–30 days, but since there are no visible signs of her receptivity, she presents her rump flirtatiously to the male. It takes a while to attract his attention, since he usually responds with a show of utter boredom; eventually, however, he takes the hint. Gorillas mate in a variety of ways. In one of the favorite positions, the male sits down and lifts the female into his lap. Alternatively, she backs into him and he crouches behind her hips. Very rarely, gorillas mate face-to-face. The coupling, which may last from 15 seconds to 20 minutes, is a vocal affair in which both sexes whimper and hoot.

Meanwhile, the atmosphere in the group may become highly charged, and excited subadult males mount nonreceptive females. Adult males may also try to mate with receptive females, and the dominant silverback often—but not always—interjects such activity. Lone silverbacks are even drawn to the group by the commotion; their presence may occasionally incur the leader's wrath, although he generally tolerates such intrusions.

Gestation lasts for about eight and a half months, after which the female gives birth lying down, and usually at night, to a single infant. Sometimes two are born, but very rarely do both survive. The mother is highly attentive to the infant, holding it to her single pair of breasts to suckle.

For the next six months she barely releases her grasp on the tiny baby. For its part, the infant can only cling to its mother's hairy belly at first, but it develops rapidly. Within a couple of months it is a lively toddler, and three or four months later it can ride on its mother's back and has the confidence to wander off and play with other infants. When the youngsters run out of games to play among themselves, they do not hesitate to clamber over adults and juveniles to pull their hair and try their patience otherwise. The adults simply put up with it all.

The young gorilla spends two and a half to three years suckling, during which time it gradually interacts more and more with other group members—regardless of their age or sex. By the time it is three or four years old, its mother may well be pregnant again; at this point the pair usually part company. If the youngster is female, she will remain in the group for a few years more. But eventually she, too, will leave for a solo male or another, smaller group where she can gain rank more rapidly and breed herself. Because of the high infant mortality, she may raise only two or three young to adulthood during her entire life. ∎

MOTHER LOVE

The infant is regularly groomed by its mother, who carefully picks off particles of fecal matter, parasites, and loose skin (below).

Baby gorillas can walk when less than a year old; like us, however, they are helpless at birth (left).

John Cancalosi/Bruce Coleman Ltd.

FROM BIRTH TO DEATH	

GORILLA

GESTATION: 8.5 MONTHS	**SEXUAL MATURITY/MALE:** 8–9 YEARS
NO. OF YOUNG: 1, RARELY 2	
WEIGHT AT BIRTH: 4.4 LB (2 KG)	**SEXUAL MATURITY/FEMALE:** 7–8 YEARS
FIRST CRAWLING: 9 WEEKS	
FIRST WALKING: 35–40 WEEKS	**LONGEVITY:** 37 YEARS IN THE WILD; MAY LIVE MORE THAN 50 YEARS IN CAPTIVITY
WEANED: 2.5–3 YEARS	
INDEPENDENT: UP TO 4.5 YEARS	

MATING

When receptive, the female incites the male to mate by thrusting her rump toward him. But gorillas are not by nature oversexed creatures, and it may take a while to break down his typically cool reserve (left).

in SIGHT

INFANTICIDE

This phenomenon is not unusual among primates and has been observed in gorillas. When a new dominant male joins a widowed group, this new male will sometimes seek to kill young infants. When infants die for any reason, their mothers come into estrus right away and become pregnant by the resident male. A new male will instinctively prefer to invest his protective efforts in his own offspring. Naturally, the females will try to counteract infanticidal behavior and often succeed.

Barry Croucher/Wildlife Art Agency

GROWING UP

The life of a young gorilla

APE CHILD

The newborn weighs about 4.4 lb (2 kg) and has sparse hair on its pinkish gray skin. It also looks eerily human—far more so than any adult ape (right).

PATERNAL PRIDE

The silverback is touchingly protective toward his tiny offspring, even taking time out to play with it (left).

A MAD, BAD REPUTATION

THE RAVENING BEAST TYPECAST IN *KING KONG* CLEARLY BEARS NO RESEMBLANCE TO REAL GORILLAS, BUT HUMANS PERSIST IN HATING, FEARING, AND EXPLOITING ONE OF THEIR CLOSEST LIVING RELATIVES

The gorilla has featured, for better or worse, in the daily life and legend of African tribes for countless generations. The chimpanzee was familiar even to the Romans, who visited Africa almost 2,500 years ago, but the gorilla has been known to the white man for only 100 years or so.

Two missionaries named Wilson and Savage, who were in the Gabon River in 1846, are credited as the first westerners to discover the gorilla. They collected several of the huge skulls, sending them back to England to the anatomists Wyman and Owen. Savage wrote that the big apes were "exceedingly ferocious, and always offensive in their habits." Owen, never even having seen a gorilla, upstaged Savage when he wrote of the unfortunate African native who stumbles across a gorilla in the forest and is "...hoisted up into the tree, uttering, perhaps, a short choking cry. In a few minutes he falls to the ground a strangled corpse."

The tall stories did not end there. In 1856 American explorer Paul du Chaillu became the first white man to shoot a gorilla. He described his hapless quarry as "some hellish dream creature—a being of that hideous order, half-man, half-beast." Notwithstanding this and similarly lurid comments, much of du Chaillu's published memoirs of his African explorations remained the most accurate account of gorillas for the next hundred years. Indeed, as the years passed, the myth of the raging beast was embellished and corroborated by other "experts" until the ignorant public, which knew no better, swallowed the lie in its entirety.

MOUNTAIN DISCOVERY

In the last decade of the 19th century, explorer Henry Stanley became convinced by rumors and reports that there were gorillas to be found in northeastern Congo. There were sightings of animals that were more likely to have been chimps, and an explorer found what was clearly a gorilla skeleton in the Virungas in 1898. But it was not until 1902 that the mountain gorilla was seen by the man in whose honor it was named. Oscar von Beringe, a German

Martin Harvey/NHPA

Poachers set thousands of snares such as these (above) *every year in the Virunga forests.*

Andrew Plumtre/Oxford Scientific Films

OUT OF ACTION

DISEASES

Gorillas suffer from many of the same afflictions that strike us, such as cancer, arthritis, and pneumonia. In fact, respiratory disorders and other diseases account for more deaths than any other factor. On the Virunga volcanoes, gorillas can easily catch colds, especially during periods of rain. In West Africa, gorillas seem to be prone to a tropical skin disease called yaws. This produces large red swellings on the face and is highly contagious. They also suffer from a disease similar to leprosy. Parasites, such as hookworm, are also common.

Next to humans, leopards are the gorilla's greatest enemy, but only a big leopard will dare tackle a silverback.

officer, was climbing on Mt. Sabinio when his party spotted gorillas; they sent a skull back to Germany, where it was identified as that of a new subspecies, *G. g. beringei*. This scientific milestone proved an unfortunate one for the newly discovered gorilla, as collectors rushed to the scene to seize their trophies. Over the ensuing quarter-century, more than fifty gorillas were shot or captured in the region.

It was not until 1959, when Americans George and Kay Schaller visited eastern Africa, that the gorilla's public image began to gain favor—and some semblance of accuracy. Schaller and his wife studied the gorilla in its habitat for several months, painstakingly assembling an account of its daily life that banished the lurid myths. It was this radically new perception of the ape that inspired Dian Fossey to make that same journey of discovery a few years later (see Miracle in the Mist page 885).

Inspired by these and other pioneering naturalists, we have at last started to protect this distant relative, but sadly the odds are now stacking against the gorilla. There are probably 30,000–40,000 western lowland gorillas, although some estimates rise as high as 100,000. Some 4,000–5,000 eastern lowland gorillas remain in the eastern Congo, while of the mountain gorillas probably only 400–650 survive.

EATING THE APE

For centuries, Africans have hunted and eaten the western lowland gorilla. These include tribes from Cameroon, Gabon, Congo, and equatorial Guinea,

Infants are at risk, too, but new laws and severe penalties for illegal trade help protect them.

ENDANGERED SPECIES

such as the Mahongwe, Sameye, Bengum, Bulu, Fang, and Mendjim Mey. Indeed, the M'Beti of Gabon relied for a long time upon the gorilla for their only source of meat. They would surround a gorilla group in the forest, fencing it in with nets lashed to trees. They then would shoot the helpless apes with old blunderbusses loaded with nuts, bolts, and shreds of tin. The Mendjim Mey displayed more courage on their hunting forays, often tackling gorillas with spears. They would scoff at the apes and deride any villager wounded by a charging silverback—only a coward who turned and ran, they maintained, could be thus injured. However, their fearless boasts compare feebly with the example set by George Schaller, who spent more than a year alone and at close range with the gorillas, carrying nothing more lethal than a pencil and notebook.

The fear with which many locals regard gorillas often leads to impulsive shootings, since firearms are becoming more widespread among the human inhabitants of gorilla country. Lone villagers who stumble upon a gorilla group unnerve the apes; to defend his group, the head silverback charges at the intruder. The charge is probably a bluff, since gorillas almost invariably stop and turn away before

---

THE WESTERN LOWLAND GORILLA'S HABITAT IS TODAY BEING ERODED BY COMMERCIAL LOGGING VENTURES

---

impact—but the villager shoots anyway, out of sheer fright. Deprived of a leader, the group often disintegrates, or else it is taken over by another silverback. For his part, the replacement boss is likely to kill any infants, since this will bring the females back into sexual receptivity and enable him to engender his own offspring. Clearly, the repercussion from the death of one male can be severe.

Gorillas are still eaten widely today—indeed, in all equatorial Africa except Uganda and Rwanda, where traditional customs forbid their consumption. The people of Congo eat some 40,000 tons of bush meat each year, and while most of this derives from bushpigs, monkeys, and antelope, they also trap or hunt about 500 gorillas, as well as numerous chimps and elephants.

Hunting of this sort has only recently started to affect the lowland gorilla's status. In years gone by, a comparatively sparse human population, spread thin over the Congo Basin, made little dent upon the ape's numbers. The gorilla probably even benefited from human activity, as villagers shifted their farms and allowed former pastures to return to secondary forest, which provides the ideal conditions for plentiful ground cover.

Anne Cree

MOUNTAIN GUERRILLAS

The plight of the mountain gorilla has touched millions of people the world over, but the

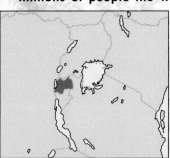

media circus sometimes obscures a human element. Rwanda, Zaire, and Uganda have all suffered some of the worst conflicts seen in Africa during the last 30–40 years.

When Belgium conceded political independence to Zaire, formerly the Belgian Congo, in 1960, opposing factions fought for control of the country. The unrest was felt even in the Virungas. Park rangers were shot down, and villagers invaded the preserve to graze their cattle. Farms and crops were burned in the utter mayhem, and hungry locals turned on the gorillas.

Uganda has suffered great civil disorder, particularly during the 1970s regime of General Idi Amin. Even before this time, the pressure of overpopulation through immigration forced the government to release one-third of its Kigezi Gorilla Sanctuary as farmland. During Amin's period of misrule, poaching was rife throughout the country.

Most recently, however, Rwanda has been hit by a terrible and bloody civil war between its two main ethnic groups, the Hutu and Tutsi. Rwanda has a long history of violence. The Tutsi were originally a racial minority ruling over the oppressed Hutu people, who formed some 90 percent of the population. Belgium ruled Rwanda from 1916–1962, during which time it tried to

---

CONSERVATION MEASURES

● The gorilla is listed in Appendix I of the Convention on International Trade in Endangered Species of Fauna and Flora (CITES). This means that unlicensed international trade in the gorilla is banned.

● The International Mountain Gorilla Project is an international body supporting Rwanda's efforts to preserve its gorillas. It was set up in 1978, and is funded today, by a joint coalition of the Fauna and Flora

introduce a measure of democracy. After a civil war in 1959 and political independence in 1962, the Hutu rebelled and drove many of the Tutsi into exile. The Tutsi tried to recover control in 1963 and 1990, failing each time. The 1994 conflict, with its dreadful loss of human life, has forced the difficult question of whether it is morally justifiable for the world to lavish concern upon a few hundred gorillas in the face of such suffering.

Surprisingly, however, it seems that the gorillas are little perturbed by the conflict raging around them. During the last civil war, only one gorilla was believed to have died, although the field research station of the Dian Fossey Foundation was ransacked. Conservationists are cautiously confident that the mountain gorillas will ride over the current human crisis with equal success.

GORILLAS IN DANGER

THIS CHART SHOWS HOW THE INTERNATIONAL UNION FOR THE CONSERVATION OF NATURE CLASSIFIES THE STATUS OF GORILLAS:

GORILLA (THE SPECIES AS A WHOLE)	VULNERABLE
MOUNTAIN GORILLA	ENDANGERED

THE MOUNTAIN GORILLA IS IN DANGER OF BECOMING EXTINCT WITHIN A CENTURY OF ITS DISCOVERY BY WESTERN SCIENTISTS. AS A SPECIES OVERALL, HOWEVER, THE GORILLA IS CONSIDERED ONLY VULNERABLE; THIS IS DUE TO THE RELATIVELY STRONG STATUS OF THE WESTERN LOWLAND GORILLA IN THE REMOTE CONGO BASIN. THERE IS, HOWEVER, NO ROOM FOR COMPLACENCY.

D. Parer & E. Parer-Cook

IT HAS WEATHERED THE WAR WELL, BUT THE MOUNTAIN GORILLA IS STILL CRITICALLY RARE.

Preservation Society, the African Wildlife Foundation, and the World Wide Fund for Nature.

● The Dian Fossey Gorilla Fund (DFGF) is a charity based in London and Rwanda. It was set up by Fossey in 1978 as the Digit Fund, named after her favorite silverback. The DFGF funds research and also supports antipoaching teams who work closely with government park wardens.

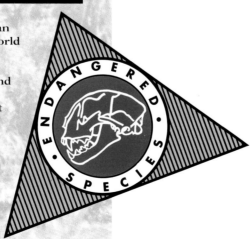

Today, however, logging means big money, especially in the form of mahogany and other hardwoods, and human impact is making its indelible mark. The logging companies carve deep into the primary forest, picking up a local workforce to suit their needs. There are invariably too few jobs to meet the insatiable demand for employment, and the unluckier locals try making a living instead from game hunting. They trap gorillas, among other mammals, and the preserved flesh is then sent back to the big towns for consumption. Historically, however, Africans cannot accept full blame here, since Europeans and North Americans have come to Africa for years simply in order to hunt gorillas. One British hunter killed 115 western lowland gorillas, and during the first half of this century visitors shot more than 60 "big game" gorillas in the Virungas.

Not all gorilla hunts are for personal gain; some are reprisal killings exacted by vengeful villagers. In many villages, the forest butts right up against the farmland, and gorillas may bed down for the night only a stone's throw away. Those apes that develop a taste for fruit—the western lowlanders in particular—cause trouble for themselves by raiding crops. Not only do they eat all the fruit from a banana tree, they also strip the trunk and eat its pith. Trees are ruined, and the furious farmers vent their fury upon any animal that they can find. Of course, the gorillas that die in the vendetta are almost certainly not those guilty of raiding the crops in the first place.

PEOPLE PRESSURE

The main impetus behind the increasing logging and hunting is a result of the population explosion occurring across most of Africa. While the lowland gorillas are more or less holding their ground in the vast and fertile Congo Basin, the mountain gorillas are trapped like fish in a barrel, surrounded by some

ALONGSIDE MAN

GORILLA WATCHING

While the chimp and its buffooning antics came to represent a cheeky caricature of humanity, the gorilla was once typecast as public enemy number one. But there is a world of difference between *King Kong* and *Gorillas in the Mist*, the Dian Fossey biopic of the 1980s. Wrongly accused for decades, the apes have at last had the chance to prove themselves quite unlike the nightmarish, slavering beast they were depicted to be.

Today, gorilla watching has moved up from the freak show to the forest. The International Mountain Gorilla Project promotes tourism, but it makes every attempt to minimize the disturbance caused to the gorillas. They permit fewer than twenty visitors to the Virungas per month, and these are limited to one hour of strictly hands-off observation.

of the densest human settlement on the continent. Although Rwandans and Ugandans do not eat the mountain apes, they do eat bush meat—and some of the last prime game forests in the region also happen to house the apes. Local poachers lay snares and spiked pits for duiker antelope and bushpigs, but all too often accidentally end up with gorillas.

Another threat today lies in the use of fetishes. These are cured animal parts collected and sold locally for their supposed magical powers. Some locals believe that a gorilla's fingers, for example,

Through her infinite patience, Dian Fossey won the respect and companionship of the mountain gorillas and was able to study their daily lifestyle (below).

when crumbled into a child's bathwater, will confer the strength of a gorilla upon the child. The Fang tribe of equatorial Guinea once believed that the brain of a gorilla could be used in charms to bring success with women. Such beliefs may seem laughable to western minds, but they are taken seriously there.

Although the entire Virunga region is officially protected as a national park, this paper decree alone will not deter hungry hunters, cattle-grazers, or collectors of honey, bamboo, and firewood. Few African governments can spare the ready cash to enforce laws that do not seem to bring benefits to their needy people. The one clear exception lies in Rwanda, where gorilla watching is finally proving its superiority, in terms of earning potential, over other, more short-term land uses.

For example, one such misguided use of the precious forests lay in a lavish project to harvest pyrethrum, a fragrant bloom of the chrysanthemum family that, when dried, can be used as a natural insecticide on crops and flowers. In the late 1960s and 1970s, the World Bank financed the deforestation of almost one-fifth of the Parc National des Volcans in Rwanda to accommodate new pyrethrum plantations. Later in the 1970s the pyrethrum market collapsed, and the short-lived plantations were abandoned. The naked ground can be farmed for a year or two—or used for cattle grazing—but the land is soon drained of its goodness, resulting ultimately in barren wasteland. ∎

INTO THE FUTURE

There is much still to find out about the plight of western lowland gorillas: They are so widespread throughout dense rain forest that their numbers cannot be accurately estimated. They do have legal protection in all the eight countries over which they roam, but enforcement is extremely difficult and is almost universally ineffective.

Enforcement is difficult also in the Virungas, particularly with the recent strife in Rwanda. Civil war is not new in this region, and conservation groups, such as the Dian Fossey Gorilla Fund (DFGF), have suffered repeated setbacks. While the gorillas have luckily suffered few direct losses, the infrastructure needed to preserve their habitat crumbles away with each new round of hostilities. In 1994 DFGF workers were hurriedly evacuated from Rwanda until it was safe to return. Miraculously, the gorilla groups under regular study

PREDICTION

MOUNTAIN RESCUE

The lowland gorillas are not in trouble at present, although inroads on their habitat may soon affect their populations. The mountain gorillas may yet survive the millenium if enough local people and governments are made to care for their future.

by the DFGF had produced four new infants, but the constant interruptions cannot help their cause.

The gorillas and the people of the Virungas depend on each other. The apes are a unique local attraction bringing a measure of prosperity and stability; if they are lost, then many human lives will be impoverished. The good news is that the new Rwandan government has pledged its commitment to protecting the volcano habitat, as it is fully aware of the star quality of its gorillas. Gorilla watching is one of Rwanda's highest-earning industries; even during the worst of the war, soldiers and reporters were pleading with wardens to be given a glimpse of the apes. Admittedly, tourism is not a universally popular notion: During the 1980s the Rwandan government wanted to push it heavily, but Dian Fossey was a staunch opponent, and it was not until after her death that tourism was set up to any degree. It is hoped that now, at the eleventh hour, those people involved can work together to provide a safe future for both gorillas and mankind. ∎

BRAZZAVILLE BABIES

Today, baby gorillas command a high price on the streets of Brazzaville and Pointe-Noire in Congo, and poachers do not flinch from killing adult gorillas just to get their hands on the youngsters.

Thankfully, however, some of these babies are confiscated by the authorities and whisked from the streets to safety. Since 1987 John Aspinall, the director of Howletts and Port Lymne Zoos in England, has been running an orphanage for young apes in the grounds of Brazzaville Zoo, Congo. The purpose of the orphanage, which has been officially sanctioned by the Congolese government, is to provide a rehabilitation center for the young apes in order that they may later be returned to the wild. To date, the center has saved the lives of more than twenty pygmy chimps and gorillas.

MIRACLE IN THE MISTS

In 1967, 35-year-old Dian Fossey set out from the United States to study gorillas in the Virungas, setting up her Karisoke Research Center on the misty slopes. For nearly two decades she lived with the gorillas, patiently earning their trust and guarding them from traps laid by game poachers. Her task was a lonely one, but in time she won worldwide respect. The sworn enemy of local poachers, she was murdered in her cabin in 1985. Many critics declaimed her as an obsessive amateur, but countless others praised her courage. Her 1983 book Gorillas in the Mist *was a groundbreaking study of wild animals; the 1987 film of the same name celebrated the extraordinary achievements of a brave and devoted woman.*

Illustration Kim Thompson

GUINEA PIGS

Jane Burton/Bruce Coleman Ltd.

UNIQUE RODENTS

THE GUINEA PIG MAY BE A FAMILIAR HOUSEHOLD PET, BUT ITS FAMILY CONNECTIONS ARE FAR FROM COMMON. IT IS A MEMBER OF A LARGE GROUP OF SOUTH AMERICAN RODENTS THAT DATES BACK MILLIONS OF YEARS

G uinea pigs mean different things to different people: They make popular pets the world over; they make docile subjects for experimentation; and to some South Americans they make for a tasty meal. But in fact, guinea pigs, or cavies (*above*), are much more than that. They are by far the most familiar members of a large group of South American rodents known as caviomorphs, or cavylike rodents, whose fossil history dates back 35 million years to a time when primitive ratlike creatures lived in what is now southern Patagonia.

Most cavylike rodents are rat sized, but some, such as the capybara, are the largest of all rodents. Some resemble small, hoofed mammals, and, as South America lacks native hoofed animals, these rodents are held to be examples of animals that might, had they not become so specialized in other ways, have evolved into creatures occupying the same ecological niches as the hoofed animals of Africa and Asia.

CLASSIFICATION

The cavylike rodents of South America are divided into five super-families, which among them contain 13 families. There are 159 species in 44 genera.

ORDER
Rodentia
(rodents)

SUBORDER
Caviomorpha
(cavylike rodents)

FIVE SUPER-FAMILIES

Cavoidea
(cavies,
pacaran,
pacas,
agoutis,
acouchis,
capybara)

Chinchilloidea
(chinchillas,
viscachas,
pacaranas)

Octodontoidea
(degus & other
octodonts,
chinchilla-rats,
tuco-tucos,
spiny rats,
hutias,
coypu)

Erethizontoidea
(New World
porcupines)

A mara suckles her youngsters (right), *sitting up meanwhile to keep a lookout for predators.*

The cavies' classification is somewhat complex! The suborder Caviomorpha contains four super-families (collections of families) of South American rodents, the largest of which is that of the Cavoidea, or cavioids. This contains three families: The true cavies (Caviidae), the pacaranas, pacas, agoutis, and acouchis (Dasyproctidae), and the capybara (Hydrochoeridae). The true cavy family contains 17 species in five genera, inlcuding the genus *Cavia* itself. There are eight *Cavia* species, found variously in Ecuador, Brazil, Peru, Argentina, Colombia, Bolivia, and Uruguay. Looking much like the famil-iar domestic guinea pig, *Cavia porcellus*, is its closest relative, the wild cavy, *Cavia aperea*.

OTHER CAVIES

Also in the cavy family are three species of mountain cavy, three yellow-toothed cavies, the rock cavy or moco, and two species of Patagonian cavy, also known as maras or Patagonian hares. Mountain cavies and yellow-toothed cavies are similar in appearance to true cavies, but they tend to be smaller and have obvious white rings around the eyes—par-ticularly the mountain cavies. The single species of rock cavy differs from the others in its habitat—it lives only among rocks in eastern Brazil, and its claws are consequently blunt rather than sharp.

Patagonian hares differ from other cavies in that they are far bigger and have longer legs, enabling them to run very fast. When resting, a mara adopts an unusual position for a rodent; it either sits on its

T. Whittaker/FLPA

John Lythgoe/Planet Earth Pictures

The paca (above) *is nocturnal, and sleeps through the day in a cozy burrow or hollow log.*

ISOLATED EVOLUTION

During the late Cretaceous period, the South American landmass, together with Antarctica and Australasia, separated from the remaining continents. By this time the marsupials were well established and for a time faced little competition from the few placental mammals that had arrived from North America.

For a time the South American marsupials coexisted with the now-evolving placentals. These placentals were very different from those elsewhere in the world, and a unique South American placental fauna was evolving, among which were the cavies and their relatives. These rodents were well established by the Miocene epoch (25–5 million years ago) and seem to have been well able to withstand competition from their northern cousins when, at the start of the Pliocene epoch, South America became linked once more to North America via the Panama land bridge. Most of the marsupials and many of the South American placentals became extinct. However, together with some of the edentates (anteaters, sloths, and armadillos), the cavylike rodents have survived and are clearly able to withstand competition from any of the North American species that attempt to invade South America.

haunches with its forelegs straight, or lies down with its forelegs tucked under its body like a cat.

The family Dasyproctidae contains eleven species of agouti and two species of acouchi, which are all more ratlike in appearance than cavies, having longer, pointed noses. The fur color varies from pale orange through brown to almost black. Their close relatives, the pacas, of which there are two species, are less ratlike, having spotted fur and blunter noses.

Chinchilloid caviomorphs include the four species of chinchilla and two kinds of viscacha. Similar in size to the cavies, these animals are distinguished by their relatively large ears, their soft fur, and long, fully furred tails. Chinchillas have an extremely dense, silky fur, with as many as sixty hairs growing out of each hair follicle. Like the guinea pigs, chinchillas are bred in captivity and many different fur colors have been produced.

The superfamily Octodontoidea contains six families; the family Octodontidae itself includes the degus, viscacha rats, and the coruro. The other five families are the tuco-tucos (Ctenomyidae), chinchilla-rats (Abrocomidae), spiny rats (Echimyidae), hutias (Capromyidae), and the coypu (Myocastoridae).

Like chinchillas, degus have large ears and long tails, but the tails are less furry. Tuco-tucos are like North American pocket gophers in appearance, which is not all that surprising as they occupy the same ecological niche. Chinchilla-rats, as their name implies, are like chinchillas but with long, pointed faces like those of rats. The spiny rats and their relatives form a large group of sixty-nine species. They have a distinctly ratlike appearance, but the coat of a spiny rat consists of stiff, sharp-pointed hairs, giving it a bristly, or spiny feel. Hutias also form a relatively large group. They are large, cavylike animals; some species are found in the West Indies. The coypu is sometimes classified in the same family as the hutias, but probably merits being placed in a family of its own.

THE TERM "GUINEA" PROBABLY DERIVES FROM THE SOUTH AMERICAN COUNTRY; "PIG" MAY REFER TO THE CAVY'S PIGLIKE SQUEALS, OR TO THE TASTE OF ITS FLESH

The superfamily Dinomyoidea contains just one family and one genus, *Dinomys*, the pacarana. "Pacarana" is an Indian name meaning false paca, and this secretive, forest-dwelling animal does quite closely resemble the pacas. However, its body is more thickset and it has a hairy tail about a quarter the length of its body.

The caviomorphs also include the family of New World porcupines (Erithizontidae), which some authorities link to the Old World porcupines (Hystricidae). As a result the caviomorphs are sometimes referred to as hystricomorph rodents. But there is much debate as to a common ancestry. ■

THE CAVIES' FAMILY TREE

Cavies and cavylike rodents, which evolved in South America, belong to the suborder Caviomorpha, within the Rodent order. Although some of the porcupines have found their way into North America and others may have been taken by humans into the Old World, the group is, by and large, unique to the native subcontinent in which it first evolved.

MARA

Dolichotis patagona

(doll-ih-COAT-iss pat-ah-GO-nah)

The mara, or Patagonian hare, is one of the most unlikely looking members of the caviomorphs: it barely resembles a rodent. It has much longer legs than its relatives, and often sits up like a dog. It lives in the thorny scrubland of central and southern Argentina, where it feeds on short grasses and herbs. Closely related is the salt desert cavy, D. salinicolum.

SQUIRREL-LIKE RODENTS

MOUSELIKE RODENTS

Color illustrations Kim Thompson

CAVY

Cavia

(*CAV-ee-ah*)

The family Caviidae, or true cavies, includes seventeen species in five genera. Included are the maras, genus Dolichotis (see left), although these are physically quite distinct from other cavies.

There are eight species in the genus Cavia. Most are dumpy with a large head, short legs, and sharp claws. They are widespread across South America, occurring in grassland, scrub, and other habitats. The wild cavy, Cavia aperea, is thought to be the ancestor of the domestic guinea pig.

OTHER SPECIES

MOUNTAIN OR DESERT CAVIES

YELLOW-TOOTHED CAVIES

ROCK CAVY

MARA OR PATAGONIAN HARE

The two chinchilla species live in the mountains of South America. Other cavylike rodents include the viscacha, coypu, hutias, pacas, agoutis, acouchis, pacarana, chinchilla-rats, spiny rats, degus, and tuco-tucos.

CAVYLIKE RODENTS

CHINCHILLA

Chinchilla

(*chin-CHIL-ah*)

ALL RODENTS

ANATOMY:
THE WILD CAVY

Cavylike rodents vary dramatically in size. Largest of the superfamily—and indeed of all the world's rodents—is the capybara, with a head-and-body length of 42–53 in (107–135 cm) and a maximum weight of 141–146 lb (64–66 kg). Smaller representatives of the caviomorphs include the degus, which have a head-and-body length of 5–8 in (13–20 cm). Chinchilla rats and tuco-tucos are also tiny.

THE EYES

are sensitive and the animal is constantly on the lookout for danger, even when eating with its head down.

THE LARGE EARS

are positioned well to the sides of the head, and can pick up the faintest sounds.

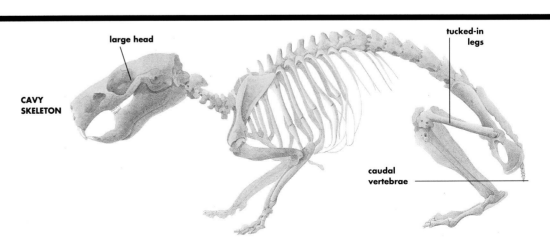

THE WHISKERS,

or vibrissae, are highly sensitive. Some cavies have whiskery eyebrows, too, to help them assess their surroundings in the dark.

THE TEETH

A cavy's incisor teeth, like those of all rodents, are designed for gnawing. However, unlike a rat's teeth, which are a yellow-brown color, a cavy's teeth are white.

SHARP CLAWS

on all four feet help the cavy clamber around. They grow continually, but are worn down on the rough ground.

Anatomy illustrations Simon Turvey/Wildlife Art Agency

The cavy sits and walks with its legs tucked under its body. Its skeleton reveals this hunched posture. There are only five to seven caudal (tail) vertebrae tucked under the pelvic girdle, hence the lack of any visible tail. The cavy's body forms a contrast with that of the Patagonian hare, which has longer legs and a more upright stance.

large head

tucked-in legs

CAVY SKELETON

caudal vertebrae

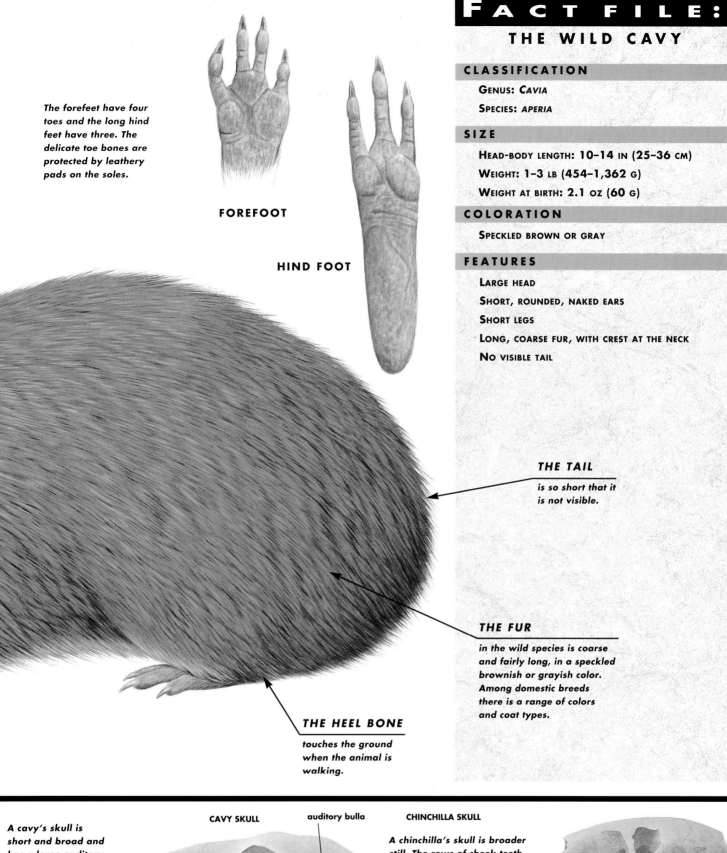

The forefeet have four toes and the long hind feet have three. The delicate toe bones are protected by leathery pads on the soles.

FOREFOOT

HIND FOOT

FACT FILE:
THE WILD CAVY

CLASSIFICATION

GENUS: *CAVIA*

SPECIES: *APERIA*

SIZE

HEAD-BODY LENGTH: 10–14 IN (25–36 CM)

WEIGHT: 1–3 LB (454–1,362 G)

WEIGHT AT BIRTH: 2.1 OZ (60 G)

COLORATION

SPECKLED BROWN OR GRAY

FEATURES

LARGE HEAD

SHORT, ROUNDED, NAKED EARS

SHORT LEGS

LONG, COARSE FUR, WITH CREST AT THE NECK

NO VISIBLE TAIL

THE TAIL
is so short that it is not visible.

THE FUR
in the wild species is coarse and fairly long, in a speckled brownish or grayish color. Among domestic breeds there is a range of colors and coat types.

THE HEEL BONE
touches the ground when the animal is walking.

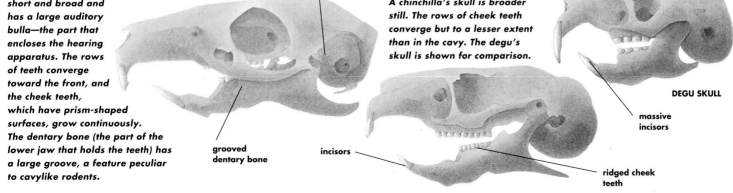

A cavy's skull is short and broad and has a large auditory bulla—the part that encloses the hearing apparatus. The rows of teeth converge toward the front, and the cheek teeth, which have prism-shaped surfaces, grow continuously. The dentary bone (the part of the lower jaw that holds the teeth) has a large groove, a feature peculiar to cavylike rodents.

CAVY SKULL

auditory bulla

grooved dentary bone

CHINCHILLA SKULL

A chinchilla's skull is broader still. The rows of cheek teeth converge but to a lesser extent than in the cavy. The degu's skull is shown for comparison.

incisors

ridged cheek teeth

DEGU SKULL

massive incisors

CAVY COLONIES

CAVIES AND THEIR RELATIVES LIKE COMPANY. THERE IS USUALLY ENOUGH FOOD TO SUPPORT A GROUP OF INDIVIDUALS—AND THERE IS SAFETY IN NUMBERS

Most rodents are highly vulnerable to attack by predators, so to increase each individual's chances of survival some cavylike species form large colonies. And in some cases, a colony will defend its territory against invaders from a nearby colony. The degree of territoriality and amount of aggression shown between individuals, however, varies according to the species.

True cavies are generally found in small groups of five to ten individuals, although in a habitat in which they thrive there may be a number of groups living in close proximity, giving the impression, at least, of a large colony. In one study the maximum population density was estimated to be 15 animals per acre (38 per hectare).

The home range of a male cavy is about 15,000 square feet (1,400 square meters), while that of a

---

TUCO-TUCO POPULATIONS AS DENSE AS 84 INDIVIDUALS PER ACRE (207 PER HECTARE) HAVE BEEN RECORDED

---

female is slightly smaller. A cavy's home range is stable and is centered around a particular clump of vegetation that is used for shelter. Because food is more scarce where mountain cavies live, their population densities tend to be smaller and individuals have larger home ranges. A male may forage over an area of over 80,500 square feet (7,500 square meters). Yellow-toothed cavies live in less arid areas and have home ranges somewhere between those of true cavies and mountain cavies.

Unlike most caviids, Patagonian hares can travel long distances. Their behavior is not at all territorial and they usually move about in groups of three or four—occasionally groups of forty have been seen. They use several forms of locomotion. In

The capybara (right) *is well suited to a watery lifestyle: Its eyes and nose are placed high on its head, so that it can submerge almost fully, while still keeping watch for predators.*

J. Bernardes/ZEFA

Jen and Des Bartlett/Bruce Coleman Ltd.

A Patagonian hare browsing on shrubs (above). *This large caviid inhabits grassland and scrub desert in central and southern Argentina.*

The territorial degu (below) *lives in small colonies in southern South America.*

addition to being able to walk, they can hop like a rabbit or hare, gallop, or "stot"—bounce on all four legs at the same time.

Cavies are active during the day, but agoutis and acouchis may be active during the day or night and pacas are nocturnal, as is the pacarana. Where agoutis have been constantly disturbed by people, they usually emerge only at dusk. They tend to lead more solitary lives than cavies, and, if danger threatens, an agouti may pause, motionless, with one foot poised in the air. Agoutis often sit with the body erect and the ankles flat on the ground, a position from which they can start to move with great speed. They are built for running and are remarkably agile and swift.

PLAINS VISCACHAS ARE SEEN AS PESTS BY FARMERS, AS THEY COMPETE WITH DOMESTIC LIVESTOCK AND RAID CROPS

Chinchillas and viscachas tend to live in large colonies. In former days when chinchillas were more numerous in the wild, they could be found in colonies of up to 100 and today a colony of plains viscachas may still contain up to 50 individuals.

Degus live in small colonies in which there is a strong territorial sense. The burrow is the center of the defended territory and the young are often reared communally by the females. However, in spite of this strong territoriality in the wild, captive animals are remarkably tolerant toward one another and individuals coexist peaceably. ■

HABITATS

Although cavylike rodents are found in other parts of the world, most members of the group are confined to South America. Within this huge subcontinent, there are, of course, an enormous variety of habitats, and caviomorphs have adapted to most of them.

LIFE IN THE UNDERGROWTH

True cavies are found in open grassland, swamps, rocky areas, and the edges of forests, and they have been found at elevations of up to 4,200 ft (1,280 m). They are difficult to study as they are active mostly at night, moving usually through well-defined tunnels in the undergrowth and sheltering in piles of brushwood or in dense thickets.

(in)SIGHT

TUCO-TUCO TUNNELS

The tuco-tuco digs a long main tunnel, with a few side passages that either end blindly or lead to feeding sites on the surface. There is a grass-lined nest chamber, usually below the level of the main tunnel, and the burrow may be shared with lizards, mice, yellow-toothed cavies, and other animals.

The tuco-tuco uses its forefeet to loosen the soil, which it sweeps away with its hind feet, and bites through any roots that it finds. One species compacts the lining of its tunnels by standing on its forefeet, walking the hind feet up the wall, urinating, and then stamping on the moistened soil.

Pacas (above) *live in underground burrows, either of their own construction or the abandoned burrows of other animals.*

Mountain cavies, as their name suggests, live in high places. Two of the three species are found only in mountain areas, but *Microcavia australis* occurs throughout Argentina; in the semiarid thornbush of central Argentina this species is, in fact, the most abundant of all the cavies. It may be active at any time of the day; it rests under bushes, digging a shallow depression in which to sleep, and is also known to dig burrows.

Yellow-toothed cavies are found in grasslands, rocky areas, and scrub in both high and low regions. They, too, are active at any time of the day or night and they dig burrows in which to rest and sleep. Large colonies are said to honeycomb the ground in the highlands of Bolivia.

The rock cavy, or moco, of Brazil lives in dry, stony areas near rocky mountains. In such places there is generally plenty of shelter available under stones or in rock fissures, but the moco sometimes excavates burrows under the stones. It rouses itself late in the afternoon to search for food both on the ground and in the trees. If disturbed while in a tree, it descends rapidly, either in a series of bounds or a single leap, to reach the safety of the rocks.

Patagonian hares, or maras, inhabit places where the grass is coarse and there are scattered shrubs. They either construct their own burrows or shelter in the abandoned burrows of other grassland inhabitants. Like most other members of the

cavy family they live on the ground. They are more active during the day, moving into the seclusion of wooded areas at night to rest.

AGOUTIS OF THE AMAZON

Agoutis occur in a variety of habitats, including forests, dense brush, and savanna. In Peru they are confined to the Amazonian area, where they are found in all parts of the low rain-forest zone and many parts of the high rain-forest zone. Their relatives, the acouchis, also appear to be restricted to the rain forests of the Amazon basin.

Pacas live in many different habitats, but seem to prefer forested areas near water. One of the two species is found in the High Andean *paramo*—the high plateau that lies between the tree line and the permanent snow line, while the other is found only in the Amazonian part of Peru. They rest during the day in burrows that they dig or find in banks or slopes, among tree roots, or under rocks.

Viscachas and chinchillas live in burrows or rocky crevices. The plains viscacha is found in the extreme south of Paraguay and in northern and central Argentina. It inhabits relatively barren parts of the pampas, but is usually well camouflaged, as

A group of young maras, belonging to probably six adult pairs, by the entrance to their communal burrow (below).

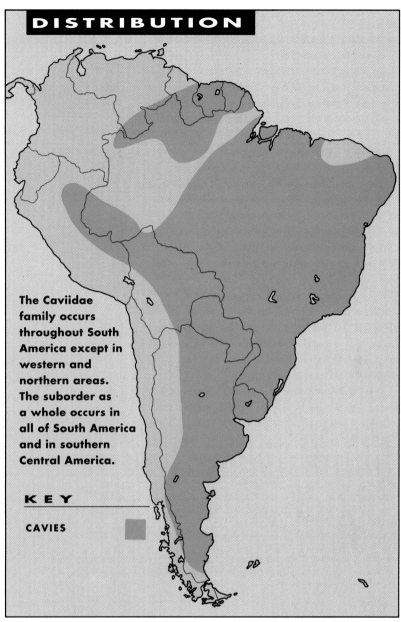

DISTRIBUTION

The Caviidae family occurs throughout South America except in western and northern areas. The suborder as a whole occurs in all of South America and in southern Central America.

KEY

CAVIES

KEY FACTS

● Plains viscachas build burrow systems, or "viscacheras," which usually consist of a large chamber about 5 ft (1.5 m) from the large entrance, with tunnels leading off in all directions. They share burrows with a variety of other animals, including toads, snakes, burrowing owls, other rodents, and skunks.

● A tuco-tuco is rarely seen outside its burrow. It generally sits in the entrance, ready to retreat at the slightest sign of danger; its naked tail appears to act as a sense organ.

● Although wild cavies are said not to burrow, there have been reports of cavies digging their own tunnels. Often they simply take over the abandoned homes of other burrowing animals.

its coloration varies with the habitat, ranging from light brown in sandy areas to gray in rocky areas.

The three mountain viscachas live in dry, rocky, mountain areas, where they run and leap among the rocks with great agility. Unlike their plains relative, they are poor diggers and are seldom found in earth burrows. Instead they live in rocky clefts, spending a large part of the day sunning and grooming themselves on the rocks.

The natural habitat of chinchillas is the relatively barren terrain found at elevations of 10,000–16,000 ft (3,000–5,000 m) in the Andes mountains. They are generally active from dusk until dawn, but they sometimes emerge on bright days to play among the rocks or simply to sit in front of their holes.

The pacarana inhabits rain forests in the valleys and lower slopes of highland regions, covering an area that extends from northwestern Venezuela and Colombia to western Bolivia. A nocturnal rodent, it shelters by day in natural crevices and holes, which it enlarges by digging. It is certainly equipped for digging as each of the four toes on its broad forefeet has long, powerful claws.

The rodents of the superfamily Octodontoidea occupy many habitat types. The degus, viscacha rats, and coruro, family Octodontidae, range from

coastal regions to elevations of over 11,500 ft (3,500 m). Tuco-tucos are found even higher, at elevations of 13,000 ft (4,000 m). Chinchilla-rats appear to be colonial animals and, again, some species are found at high altitudes. Spiny rats are generally found in forests, often near coasts and waterways; some species live on the ground, while others spend their lives in trees. Hutias are woodland animals and are found in forests and plantations. They are among the few caviomorphs found outside South America and there are species in Cuba, Jamaica, the Bahamas, and Hispaniola. ∎

898

FOCUS ON

THE PAMPAS AND CHACO

The Argentinian pampas is a temperate grassland. Almost treeless, this ocean of waving stems covers a part of the huge plains of southern South America. These plains were built up from compacted layers of soil washed down from the Andes by rivers and streams. Very few large mammals are found here, but rodents abound, including cavies, Patagonian hares, viscachas, and tuco-tucos.

Stretching from the pampas toward the mountains in the west, and the Amazon basin in the north, the chaco is an intermediate zone of lowland plains, swamps, deciduous forests, and scrub.

TEMPERATURE AND RAINFALL

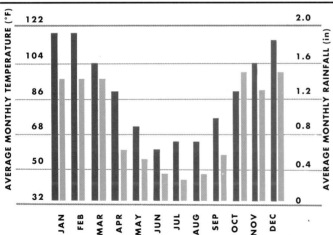

■ TEMPERATURE
▨ RAINFALL

The climate varies greatly across the chaco and pampas. The chaco is dry for much of the year, but may be heavily flooded in the rainy season. The western pampas is hot and dry, but the eastern grasslands benefit from cool, moist Atlantic winds.

NEIGHBORS

Many of these animals live in the chaco, exploiting the various watery, tree-studded, or scrubby habitats. Some regularly invade neighboring zones such as the pampas.

BUSH DOG

This elusive inhabitant of South and Central America hunts in packs and is an agile swimmer.

RIVER OTTER

The huge network of river systems in the chaco is a perfect habitat for the southern river otter.

Illustrations Edwina Goldstone/Wildlife Art Agency

ENEMIES

PAMPAS AND CHACO

The pampas stretches from Buenos Aires in the east of Argentina, west toward the Andes. The chaco extends west to the Andean foothills, and north into Paraguay and Bolivia, to the Amazon basin in Brazil.

RIO DE JANEIRO
SAO PAULO

◼ CHACO

◼ PAMPAS

EXTREMELY DANGEROUS

MARGAY
Known also as the "tigrillo," this small cat preys on rodents, monkeys, and birds in forest and scrubland.

EXTREMELY DANGEROUS

PUMA
The puma makes its home in almost any habitat it chooses. Its prey ranges from rodents to deer.

BRAZILIAN TAPIR

The tapir is a solitary creature, emerging from deep cover at night to feed on leaves and fallen fruit.

CHACOAN PECCARY

Only rediscovered in 1975, this piglike species is a true resident of the chaco. It is armed with deadly tusks.

WHITE-TAILED DEER

The most widespread deer in the American continent, its white tail acts as a danger signal.

GIANT ARMADILLO

This heavily armored animal feeds on ants and termites, and can weigh up to 100 lb (45 kg).

CARACARA

Caracaras feed on carrion in open country. Unlike other falcons, they build their own nests.

SOCIAL STRUCTURE

Within a group of cavies there is a well-defined hierarchy, with that of the males being quite separate from that of the females. Each cavy has its place within the pecking order, and when two individuals meet, the subordinate must either retreat or be attacked. If an alpha male loses its position by being defeated by a previously subordinate male, it becomes passive and withdrawn, and may even die.

A MOUNTAIN CAVY WILL "TIST" WHEN ALARMED, TWITTER WHEN ANNOYED, AND SHRIEK WHEN FRIGHTENED

Among male mountain cavies a similar hierarchy is established, but females tend to stay in a relatively small area and therefore meet other females less often. The home ranges of the males invariably overlap with those of other males, and when two males meet there is nearly always a fight—sometimes to the death. By contrast, females may kiss when they meet, particularly if they are mother and daughter, and then forage or sit together.

Yellow-toothed cavies have been studied both in the wild and in captivity, and it has been shown that two males cannot be kept together in the same pen. In the wild, aggressive displays and fights,

Jane Burton/Bruce Coleman Ltd.

A family group of chinchillas of the Peruvian Andes (above).

MALE AND FEMALE *chinchillas pull each other's fur out as part of courtship. The female is larger than the male.*

VOCALIZATION

Cavylike rodents often use sounds to communicate with each other and a large number of sounds have been identified. Cavies, for example, squeak when they are excited, chirp when they are anxious, and issue threats with a tooth chatter.

Yellow-toothed cavies indicate sexual arousal with a "churr." They, too, use teeth chattering to threaten and, during an attack, they produce a screech that sounds like a rusty gate being opened.

The rock cavy, or moco, includes whistles among the sounds it makes; a slow whistle is produced when an animal leaves the rocks in order to forage, and the alarm whistle that indicates danger is recognized by all the animals within earshot.

The most common sound produced by a plains viscacha is an "uh-huh" when it is investigating something.

Illustration Evi Antoniou

There are two species of acouchi: red and green. A young green acouchi (right) *in Amazonia.*

often resulting in serious wounds, are common, as the males strive for position in a similar type of dominance hierarchy to that shown by true cavies. Aggression is not shown toward immature individuals until they are one month old, but at this stage they can expect to be chased.

Male plains viscachas are thought to live apart from the main colony at certain times of the year, especially just before and after the young are born. Most of the time they tolerate one another, but at the onset of the breeding season they become more

---

A PLAINS VISCACHA SHOWS AGGRESSION BY STAMPING ITS FEET, WAGGING ITS TAIL, AND MAKING HIGH-PITCHED WHINES

---

aggressive and fights occur frequently. Most male chinchillas bear the scars of wounds inflicted during such fights, and deaths are not uncommon.

MAKE LOVE NOT WAR!

Mountain viscachas, however, are more peaceable. There is no serious fighting between individuals or groups, and all that happens during the breeding season is that the males become promiscuous. Competition probably exists at the sperm level.

Chinchillas appear to have similar behavior. They are sometimes said to be monogamous, and this is not unlikely since there are numerous examples of monogamy within colony social structures. Female chinchillas are very aggressive toward one another and, curiously, toward males, even when in estrus.

In spite of the fact

Rod Williams/Bruce Coleman Ltd.

RUMP-ROLLING

in sand forms part of the chinchillas' grooming session. Eating leaves heavy with dew provides them with water.

that male Patagonian hares are not territorial in their behavior, they do have a linear dominance hierarchy that is maintained by aggression. The basic social unit among Patagonian hares is the mated pair and they are strictly monogamous throughout the year.

The same is also true of agoutis, which remain together until one of the pair dies. Each pair occupies a territory, which includes several sleeping places, food trees, and natal nests. Intruding agoutis are driven off aggressively, especially by the male, and if a fight develops it is often vicious and may result in severe wounds. ∎

FOOD AND FEEDING

Like all rodents, caviomorphs are herbivores. Most species eat whatever plant food is available, which means that their diet is restricted only by the plants that grow in a particular region.

Rodents, such as cavies, viscachas, tuco-tucos, and maras, that inhabit the pampas and other South American grasslands, feed mostly on grasses, herbs, and seeds. On the pampas, cavies and plains viscachas generally feed at dusk and just before dawn, when they are least likely to be seen by predators. In cold weather, however, they may continue to feed throughout the day.

It is thought that tuco-tucos, which include roots in their diet, may pull most of their food down into their burrows from below as they appear only to make short forays onto the surface on sunny days.

SEARCHING FOR FOOD

In mountain regions food is more scarce, and rodents have to spend more of their time searching for something to eat. The mountain cavy of Argentina, for example, feeds during the day and night. Its diet consists mostly of leaves and fruit, and

VISCACHAS

eat grasses and other plants, such as lichens and moss.

Illustration Wildlife Art Agency

in SIGHT

BURIED AND LOST

Studies of agoutis and acouchis have shown that they perform a useful service to the fruit trees on which they feed. When fruit is plentiful, these rodents bury the seeds in scattered sites, so that they can dig them up when fruits are not in season. Inevitably, some sites get forgotten and the seeds germinate.

MARAS *inhabit the South American pampas, where they eat a diet of grasses, herbs, and seeds.*

902

Martin Wendler/NHPA

Rain-forest rodents, such as the agouti (left), *live on a diet of fruit, leaves, and tender stems.*

it sometimes climbs bushes and low trees to feed. It has never been seen to drink, presumably getting all the water it needs from succulent plants. Mountain viscachas eat almost any kind of plant, including lichens and moss. Chinchillas, too, eat whatever they can find and they eat by sitting erect, holding their food in their forepaws. During the dry season degus supplement their diet with fresh droppings of cattle and horses. They also store food for winter use and sometimes raid orchards, vineyards, and wheat fields for food.

The coruro of central Chile stores bulbs and tubers in its burrows. Normally, it is animals that raid human stores of food, but in this case the tables are turned, as local people raid the coruros' food stores to supplement their diet!

Most hutias feed on leaves, bark, and fruit, but one of the Cuban hutias preys on lizards and other small animals. ∎

AGOUTIS
*are mainly herbivores,
but from time to time
they may also eat young
birds, small rodents, or
large insects.*

903

REPRODUCTION

PATH BLOCKING
*by the male rock cavy
marks the beginning of
the mating game.*

True cavies produce about five litters each year. Females come into season immediately after giving birth, as do many caviomorphs. When a pregnant cavy is about to give birth, males start to gather around her; time is precious, as she will only remain receptive for half a day. The dominant male guards her jealously and generally mates with her first. But if he cannot protect her from the others, she is pursued and mated by several more males.

Gestation periods among true cavies range from 56 to 74 days. Wild cavies produce up to five young, which are well developed at birth and weigh around 2 oz (57 g). They can run about and eat solid food within hours of birth. They normally suckle for three weeks but can survive on their own after just five days. Males usually become sexually mature after three months and females after two.

In yellow-toothed cavies the estrus cycle is triggered only if there is a male present. He follows his mate around with his chin on her rump to induce her to come into season. Gestation takes 49–60 days, and up to seven well-developed young are born.

CAVIES

*live in colonies, but males
have few parental
duties.*

Illustration Joanne Cowne

904

in S I G H T

KEEPING UP NUMBERS

As with many rodents, cavies and their relatives are prolific breeders. Many are taken by predators, so plenty of offspring are needed to sustain populations. Those species that live in warm or mild climates can produce young all year round, although births generally peak in the spring (September to December in South America) to coincide with the maximum growth of grass. In hard winters breeding may cease for a time.

Chinchillas breed from May to November in the Southern Hemisphere (in the north they breed from November to May) and usually produce two, sometimes three, litters. Like cavies, they come into season immediately after giving birth. Between one and six young are born after about 110 days; they weigh about 1.2 oz (34 g), are fully furred, and have their eyes open.

Agoutis appear to breed throughout the year, although seasonal breeding has been observed in some captive agoutis. Agoutis have a courtship ritual in which the male sprays the female with his urine. This causes her to perform a lively display that can best be termed a "frenzy dance"; she allows the male to approach her only after being sprayed several times. After a gestation period of 104–120 days, the litter of one or two, occasionally three, young are born. The young can run within an hour of being born. ∎

PASSING UNDER the female's chin, the male then turns around and starts to mount her.

VISCACHA MATING PATTERNS

Location appears to play an important part in the mating patterns of the mountain viscacha *(right)*. The Peruvian species mates in October, whereas the species found in the colder climate of southern Argentina mates in May or June. Gestation takes about 140 days and there is usually only one offspring, which is born fully furred.

A female plains viscacha usually has two litters a year in the wild, although it is capable of breeding all year round in captivity. The estrus cycle lasts 45 days, and females rarely come into season again until after the young are weaned. After a gestation period of about 154 days, between one and four young are born.

Gunter Ziesler/Bruce Coleman Ltd.

RARE RODENTS

THE SOUTH AMERICAN HABITATS OF THE CAVIOMORPHS ARE FAST SUCCUMBING TO TARMAC AND THE PLOW. LIFE IS HARD ENOUGH FOR THE HUMAN POPULATION, LET ALONE A HANDFUL OF UNLOVED RODENTS

Rodents are not universally popular animals. Although rats, mice, and gerbils are widely kept as pets, many people profess to be afraid of mice, and rats have been a symbol of unpleasantness since the earliest times. This, together with their habit of raiding human food stores and their tendency to carry disease, has won them little respect from mankind, and it says much for these rodents' powers of survival that they have successfully resisted all attempts to exterminate them.

Attitudes toward cavies and their relatives, on the other hand, are somewhat different. Guinea pigs, although their features are sufficiently ratlike to unnerve people with a real fear of rodents, are generally thought of as more acceptable animals—and indeed, they make charming pets. A few species, such as the mountain cavy, the plains viscacha, and the pacas are regarded as agricultural pests because of the damage they can do, but by and large caviomorph rodents do not get a bad press.

Unfortunately, this by itself is not always sufficient to ensure their survival. Some species are present in sufficiently large numbers to make them reasonably secure for the present. The wild cavy, for example, is an adaptable animal that lives in such a wide range of habitats that it is not in any immediate danger. But most hutias, for example, are under threat, and other species have only recently become extinct.

HOMELESS AND PERSECUTED

The major problem with caviomorph conservation lies in the fact that we know so little about them. Rodents represent the largest group of mammals in South America, yet they are also the least understood. Many are tiny, most are secretive and nocturnal, and their habitats tend to be remote. Relatively few caviomorphs are officially listed as rare to any degree—not because the order as a whole is faring well, but because there is simply too little information. Furthermore, although some species may face extinction in one country, they may remain numerous in another, and consequently receive an "Indeterminate" rarity status (see page 909). Such is the case, for example, of the chinchilla.

What is known, however, is that problems facing these rodents narrow down to three main areas: persecution as pests; hunting for food or sport; and habitat loss or disturbance. In South America, land is lost every year to development for housing or industry, agriculture, timber extraction, mining, and drilling for oil. Habitats have in many cases been

The mountain viscacha (right) *is in no imminent danger of extinction, despite being hunted heavily for its flesh and fur.*

Little is known about the shy pacarana (above). *It is, however, hunted for food, both by humans and by natural predators such as jaguars and ocelots.*

This chart shows the presumed current range of the chinchillas.

RANGE OF CHINCHILLAS

The long-tailed chinchilla is found only on shrubby, north-facing slopes in the coastal Andes ranges of northern Chile. The short-tailed chinchilla is believed to live in the Andes mountains of Peru, Bolivia, and northwestern Argentina at altitudes of 4,900–8,200 ft (1,500–2,500 m); sightings are, however, very rare. Slaughtered for centuries for their fine pelts, they received protection as early as 1910—too late, though, to save them in the wild in many areas.

further degraded by the introduction of alien animal species, which either prey on native wildlife or compete for food.

In Peru and other regions, hunted wild animals provide more than three-quarters of the protein volume in the human diet—and rodents yield a significant proportion of this amount. Isolated populations of, for example, agoutis and rock cavies, have been hunted to extinction in order to fill the cooking pot. It is hard to condemn such actions when the local people have little else to eat, and the rodents in question are sharing pasture with domestic livestock.

Animals that are viewed as pests often suffer repeated attempts to exterminate them. But not all species succumb to such pressure, and it is very often the adaptability of such animals that both makes them pests and ensures their survival, as

907

long as their habitat remains intact. Others, however, are more vulnerable and most of the cavylike rodents that are considered to be pests come into this category.

The plains viscacha is a good example. Although this animal is widely liked and is often reared as a pet, it does a great deal of damage in the wild. Not only does it feed on crops and compete with domestic livestock for food, but its urine is also highly acidic, causing long-term soil degradation. Because of this, and the fact that its flesh and fur are both highly prized, the viscacha is intensively hunted. It used to occur in huge numbers on the pampas, and it is said that a person could once ride 500 mi (800 km) without ever being out of sight of a viscacha. Systematic extermination campaigns, however, have greatly reduced numbers in recent years and there are fears that this species could become extinct before the year 2000.

The mountain viscacha, too, is hunted for its meat and fur and, consequently, its numbers have declined in some areas. Between 1972 and 1979, for example, more than a million pelts were exported from Argentina. In Chile this species is protected by law, except in the north, where it is

---

IT IS ESTIMATED THAT TEN PLAINS
VISCACHAS DEVOUR AS MUCH PASTURE
AS A SINGLE DOMESTIC SHEEP

---

still abundant. However, illegal hunting continues, to the detriment of the viscacha. The mountain cavy is another target of the hunters; it, too, is considered to be good to eat and is said to destroy crops and to dig holes that are a hazard to horses. But despite being persecuted, it has adapted well to living alongside humans and, unlike the viscachas, appears to be in no danger of extinction.

Tuco-tucos, on the other hand, have not fared so well. They, too, can make horse riding hazardous with their burrow systems. In addition they sometimes damage crops and compete with domestic livestock for forage. As a result they have been intensively persecuted and their numbers have been greatly reduced in some places. There is, for example, in southern Patagonia, a large area that was once home to many tuco-tucos. Today, it is fenced off and devoted to sheep; very few tuco-tucos survive there today. Elsewhere intensive grazing by sheep and other farming practices have contributed to the decline of tuco-tucos. Many of the 44 species are now rare or endangered.

The coypu presents an ironic case: it was introduced to North America and Eurasia, where it

HUTIAS

Hutias are now seriously endangered. On the island of Cuba, their status has worsened as a result of hunting, combined with habitat destruction and predation by introduced species. The hutias themselves are not popular with humans, as many live in plantations, where they include bark and fruit in their diet.

Four of the Cuban hutias are known to scientists only from the remains of skeletons; they are presumed to be extinct. Many remains were found along with evidence of human habitation; hutias are therefore thought to have long been part of the diet of local people—some species probably disappeared before the arrival of Europeans. The decline of the remaining species was probably accelerated as the demand for meat increased, forests were cleared, and alien predators, such as the Burmese mongoose, were introduced. One species of Cuban hutia is still relatively common, and can even be hunted in a restricted annual season, but all other remaining species of Cuban hutia may be close to extinction.

The story is similar in the Bahamas, Jamaica, and Hispaniola. On these islands, most species are known only from their skeletal remains. The only Bahaman species known to exist today is classified by the International Union for the

HUTIAS (*RIGHT*) HAVE BEEN BRED WITH SOME SUCCESS IN CAPTIVITY, BUT FOR MOST SPECIES LIFE IN THE WILD IS FRAUGHT WITH HAZARDS.

CONSERVATION MEASURES

● The two species of Hispaniolan hutia receive protection in the Dominican Republic (on the eastern half of the island).

● All species of hutia are protected in certain parts of Cuba, where the cays (islands) are official wildlife protection areas.

● In the Bahamas, the subspecies *Geocapromys ingrahami ingrahami* has been introduced onto an island in the Exuma National Sea and Land Park.

Conservation of Nature (IUCN) as vulnerable. Two of its subspecies probably became extinct in earlier colonial times on the islands. A third subspecies, however, seems to be in better shape; its tiny island home of East Plana Cay remained uninhabited by humans until 1891, and today there may be as many as 12,000 animals living there. The subspecies has also been introduced to a small protected island nearby, where its numbers have risen in recent years.

The Jamaican species is rare, but fortunately a program of captive breeding and reintroduction is being carried out, and these animals are more common than was once feared. Another species that existed only on Little Swan Island off northeastern Honduras is thought to have been wiped out by a hurricane in 1955 and by the later introduction of domestic cats. The two surviving hutia species on Hispaniola are losing ground steadily against human encroachment on their forest habitat, coupled with predation by mongooses.

Inset Phillip Coffey/JWPT

● During the 1980s, the Jersey Wildlife Preservation Trust conducted a successful captive-breeding program with Jamaican hutias. They later returned the stock to Jamaica, where the animals were reintroduced into the wild. The program was executed in collaboration with Hope Zoo in Jamaica, which to this day continues to breed hutias for release.

CAVIIDS IN DANGER

THE INTERNATIONAL UNION FOR THE CONSERVATION OF NATURE (IUCN), OR THE WORLD CONSERVATION UNION, LISTS THE FOLLOWING CAVIOMORPH SPECIES IN ITS 1994 *RED DATA BOOK*:

PACARANA, CABRERA'S HUTIA, LARGE-EARED HUTIA, GARRIDO'S HUTIA, DWARF HUTIA, LITTLE EARTH HUTIA	ENDANGERED
THIN-SPINED PORCUPINE, RED VISCACHA RAT	VULNERABLE
BUSHY-TAILED HUTIA, BAHAMIAN HUTIA, HISPANIOLAN HUTIA	RARE
SHORT-TAILED CHINCHILLA, LONG-TAILED CHINCHILLA, CHAPMAN'S PREHENSILE-TAILED HUTIA, ISLA DE LA JUVENTUD HUTIA, JAMAICA HUTIA	INDETERMINATE

ZEFA

seems to be flourishing, while its native populations are suffering great losses—mainly at the hands of fur traders. It has been exploited intensely for more than 150 years; in the 1970s, Argentina exported some 25 million coypu pelts with a total value of more than $63 million. During the 1980s, the coypu constituted 50 percent of total mammal-skin exports from Argentina.

THE CHINCHILLA INDUSTRY

Chinchillas are prized for their beautiful fur, and ever since Europeans arrived in South America and demand for this fur grew, the wild chinchilla population has slumped. In the 1900s some 500,000 chinchilla skins were being exported each year. Shortly after this the numbers had fallen to such a point that chinchillas became rare and the price of their skins rose accordingly. Taking into account its size and weight, a chinchilla pelt became the most valuable pelt in the world, and at one stage coats made of wild chinchilla fur were selling for as much as $100,000 each.

Chinchillas are now protected by law in their natural habitat, but because the areas in which they live are so remote, enforcement of the law is difficult. Other reasons for their continued decline include the burning and harvesting of the algarrobilla shrub, overgrazing by domestic livestock, mining, and possibly competition with other caviomorphs, such as degus and chinchilla-rats.

Pacas attack a number of different crops; they

ALONGSIDE MAN

PETS AND LABS

Guinea pigs have been kept as pets by the Peruvian Indians for at least 3,000 years. The South American Indians also ate guinea pigs, and in some mountain regions they are still used for sacrifices.

From about 1200 to the arrival of the Spanish in 1532, the Inca Indians bred many different strains. The guinea pig was later brought to Europe, and since the mid-19th century it has been used worldwide in the study of genetics, pathology, nutrition, and other sciences.

Eric and David Hosking/FLPA

are killed in large numbers both because of this and for their reputedly tasty flesh; locally, their meat commands a higher price than any other, whether from a domestic animal or a wild species. As a result of hunting and habitat destruction, pacas are either being exterminated or becoming rare over large areas. The same causal factors have spelled trouble for the chinchilla-rats in Chile. Natives sell their pelts as chinchilla pelts to gullible travelers.

Agoutis are hunted for sport as well as for food. However, their status is not well understood. Little, too, is known about the pacarana; it was not discovered until 1873, and has always appeared to be rare. There are a number in captivity, but the wild population is thought to be on the decline as a result

Smoke billows over a South American forest as trees are cleared to make way for a road. Despite global concern, the destruction continues unabated.

Chinchillas are more common in pet shops than in their natural habitat (below).

of excessive hunting by local people and the destruction of its high-altitude rain-forest habitat.

Habitat destruction alone can be a major problem for some of the more specialized caviomorphs. The rock cavy poses no threat to humans, nor is it hunted for food. But it, too, is under threat, simply because its limited habitat is being removed. One of the two species of Patagonian hare, *Dolichotis patagona*, is now rare in the province of Buenos Aires in Argentina, where formerly it was present in large numbers. Again, habitat destruction is the main cause, but in this case it is aided by competition with the introduced and more adaptable European hare.

KNOWN BY THEIR BONES

There are a number of species known only from remains that have been found. The family Heptaxodontidae, for example, are all now thought to be extinct and, although some clearly died out before the arrival of humans, others survived until relatively recently. The species *Elasomdontomys obliquus*, for example, lived throughout the forests of Puerto Rico, but died out at about the time the first European explorers arrived. The quemi, *Quemesia gravis*, was used as a source of food by the natives of Hispaniola, but it became extinct during the first half of the 16th century.

There is, however, some hope for the capybaras in Venezuela. Here, there has for nearly 500 years been a demand for capybara meat, and its hide also provides high-grade leather. Ranchers manage the capybaras on irrigated savannas, and cull the animals in February, when breeding is at a low ebb. The rodents do not compete with cattle for pastures, since they eat shorter, succulent pastures whereas the livestock prefer taller, drier foodstuff. It may be a far cry from life in the wild, but the species has at least some human protection. ∎

Jane Burton/Bruce Coleman Ltd.

INTO THE FUTURE

The outlook for most of the South American caviomorph rodents does not seem very bright. Many of the countries involved are poor, and the conservation of any species, let alone rodents, comes second to providing for the human population. The people of South America naturally aspire to a better standard of living, and it is not surprising that the development strategies of South American governments do not, as yet, cater to their local wildlife. We may regret this, but we can hardly condemn the South Americans for wishing to improve their standard of living, particularly since we have achieved our modern way of life by drastically altering our own natural environments, albeit over a long period of time; little is left of our ancient forests and grasslands.

PREDICTION

RESEARCH AND ACTION ARE ESSENTIAL

Too little is known about caviomorphs, but most species are in serious trouble. Unless drastic steps are taken to save enough of their natural habitats and, in some cases, to develop captive-breeding programs, many will become extinct.

Another problem is the serious lack of understanding of South American rodents, which makes it difficult for conservationists to argue convincingly in favor of legislation. Such conservation legislation as there is lacks any ecological basis, and in any case is not enforced. Even where hunting is illegal, people still rely on it in order to feed, so they are hardly likely to cease hunting just to comply with the law.

Against the conservationists are powerful economic interests, such as agriculture, mining, and the fur trade. Large companies can easily outpace the conservation efforts of governments, and the degradation of South American habitats seems likely to continue, with the consequent loss of wildlife—much of which has yet to be discovered. ■

WWF CHINCHILLA PROJECT

Although chinchillas have been legally protected in Chile since 1929, they have been hunted to near extinction and now exist only in a small area in the coastal mountains. The World Wide Fund for Nature (WWF) is now establishing a reserve to protect them.

A 10,000-acre (4,300-hectare) Chinchilla National Reserve was established in 1984. Game wardens and other staff were recruited and buildings were constructed. When completed, a 26-mi (42-km) perimeter fence will exclude goats, which are thought to threaten the chinchillas because they compete for food and destroy the habitat in the process. A nursery has been established in order to grow native trees for reestablishing in the area. Patrols will be organized to prevent illegal grazing and collection of wood for fuel.

Biologists are using the reserve to monitor the chinchillas' population dynamics, their use of home ranges, their predators, and their social structure and interaction with other species. Through analysis of fecal pellets, scientists are also studying what the chinchillas eat—and how they affect the local vegetation. Special traps are used to capture chinchillas; trapped animals are marked with ear tags, and their footprints are also identified and later monitored. Radio transmitters may soon be used.

Meanwhile the search continues for other colonies. So far, two small colonies have been located within 6 mi (10 km) of the reserve and another 125 mi (200 km) to the north. Plans are being discussed to introduce chinchillas to new habitats. Without this help, there is little doubt that this animal would become extinct.

Nick Pike/Wildlife Art Agency

INDEX

Published by Marshall Cavendish Corporation
99 White Plains Road
Tarrytown, New York 10591-9001

© Marshall Cavendish Corporation, 1997
© Marshall Cavendish Ltd, 1994

The material in this series was first published in the English language by Marshall Cavendish Limited, of 119 Wardour Street, London W1V 3TD, England.

Library of Congress Cataloging-in-Publication Data

Encyclopedia of mammals.
    p. cm.
    Includes index.
    ISBN 0-7614-0575-5 (set)   ISBN 0-7614-0581-X (v. 6)

    Summary: Detailed articles cover the history, anatomy, feeding habits, social structure, reproduction, territory,
        and current status of ninety-five mammals around the world.
    1. Mammals—Encyclopedias, Juvenile. [l. Mammals—Encyclopedias.]   I. Marshall Cavendish Corporation.
    QL706.2.E54 1996
    599'.003—dc20   96-17736
                                                                              CIP
                                                                              AC

Printed in Malaysia
Bound in U.S.A.